D1568294

New Public Administration

New Public Administration

H. George Frederickson

The University of Alabama Press
University, Alabama

066 806

Library of Congress Cataloging in Publication Data

Frederickson, H. George.

New public administration.

Based on lectures sponsored by the Bureau of Public
Administration and presented at the University of
Alabama in Oct., 1977.
  Bibliography: p.
  Includes index.
  1. Public administration. I. Title.
  JF1351.F73   350   80-10569
  ISBN 0-8173-0040-6
  ISBN 0-8173-0041-4 pbk.

JF
1351
.F73
1980

Contents

Tables and Figures

Acknowledgments

This book is an accumulation of ideas, thoughts, and opinions that have been greatly and positively influenced by my teachers, my colleagues, and my students. Certain of my teachers were especially influential: Stewart Grow, Jesse Reeder, and Robert Riggs of Brigham Young University; Vincent Ostrom of Indiana University; Winston Crouch and John Bollens of the University of California at Los Angeles; Peter Woll of Brandeis University; Frank Sherwood, Elmer K. Nelson, Bruce Storm, and the late John Pfiffner of the University of Southern California; Harry Reynolds of the University of Nebraska at Omaha; and Arvo Van Alstyne of the University of Utah.

Among my colleagues over the years who have been especially helpful, most particularly are Steven K. Bailey of Harvard University; Harlan Cleveland of the Aspen Institute; Dwight Waldo, Guthrie Birkhead, Jesse Burkhead, Seymour Sacks, Henry Lambright, and John C. Honey of the Maxwell School, Syracuse University; Douglas Rae of Yale University; Charles Wise, Charles Bonser, Louis C. Gawthrop, York Wilburn, John Ryan, Donald Klingner, and Eugene McGregor of Indiana University; George Nicholas and Leo Cram of the University of Missouri; Keith Quincy, Henry Kass, Robert Herold, Shane Mahoney, George Durrie, Lawrence Kiser, Neal Zimmerman, and Edward Connerly of Eastern Washington University; Alan K. Campbell and Gilda Jacobs of the U.S. Office of Personnel Management; Frank Marini of San Diego State University; Yong Hyo Cho of the University of Akron; Kenneth Howard of the State of Wisconsin; Michael Harmon, Stephen Chitwood, and David Porter of the George Washington University; Lee Fritschler, Robert Cleary, Howard McCurdy, and Dwight Ink of the American University; Orion White, Robert Deland, and Deil Wright of the University of North Carolina, Chapel Hill; James Soles of the University of Delaware; Jong S. Jun, Carl Bellone, and Ethan Singer of the California State University at Hayward; Robert Biller, Chester Newland, Randy Harrison, Ross Clayton, Louis Weschler, Michael White, Larry Kirkhart, and John Kirlin of the University of Southern California; Margaret Conway, Conley Dillon, and Charles Levine of the University of Maryland; Charles Norris of the County of Los Angeles; Randy Hamilton of Golden Gate University; Adam Herbert of Florida International University; Howard Hallman of the Center for Governmental Studies; Thomas Vocino of Auburn University; Ray Remy of the City of Los Angeles; Mel Powell and Alden J. Stevens of Long Beach State University; John E. Kerrigan of the University of Nebraska at Omaha; Dona Wolfe of the U.S. National Credit Union Administration; Philip J. Rutledge of the National Public Management Institute; Dallin Oaks, Karl Snow, Kent Colton, Stanley Taylor, William Timmons, and Dale Williams of Brigham Young University; David K. Hart and William G. Scott of the University of Washington.

Three very special people associated with the Bureau of Public Administration of The University of Alabama, and their distinguished Lectures in Public Administration series, Colemon Ransome, Robert Highsaw, and Joseph Pilegge, were extremely helpful in arranging the lectures and the subsequent preparation of this book. Thank you for an exciting challenge and a new experience.

PERMISSIONS

Parts of Chapter 1 previously appeared as "Organization Theory and New Public Administration," Frank Marini, ed., *Toward a New Public Administration: The Minnow-brook Perspective* (San Francisco: Chandler Publishing Co., 1971). My thanks to Harper & Row Publishers, Inc., and to Linda S. Rogers for permission to reprint portions of that essay. Parts of Chapter 1 and Chapter 4 previously appeared

in "Public Administration in the 1970s: Developments and
Directions," *Public Administration Review*, 34 (September–
October 1976), 564–576. My thanks to the American Society
for Public Administration for permission to reprint portions
of that publication. Parts of Chapter 5 previously appeared
in pamphlet form in "The Recovery of Structure in Public
Administration" (Washington, D.C.: The Center for Governmental Studies, 1970). My sincere appreciation to
Howard W. Hallman of the Center for permission to use
part of that pamphlet in this book. Parts of Chapter 2
originally appeared as "The Lineage of New Public Administration," *Administration and Society*, 7 (August 1976),
149–174. My thanks to George and Sara McCune of Sage
Publications, Inc., for their permission.

Foreword

This book is generally about public administration and particularly about new public administration.

New public administration is a product of the late 1960s and the 1970s, an era characterized by Dwight Waldo as a "time of turbulence." During this period, I was teaching public administration in the Maxwell Graduate School of Citizenship and Public Affairs of Syracuse University. My courses were budgeting, policy analysis, and personnel; my job was to prepare graduate students for careers in public service. My students were hostile and angry; they were a product of the challenges and protests of the time—the turbulence. They claimed that public administration was irrelevant, out of touch with current critical issues and problems. They were right. It was in this context that I was involved with many others in the development of what has come to be known as new public administration.

Although the general context of the development of new public administration was important, several events influenced the emergence of this "movement." First, most of the major theorists, authors, and leaders in the field of public administration were invited to a conference in late 1967 sponsored by the American Academy of Political and Social Science. The chairman of the conference, James C. Charlesworth, described the purposes and mood of the conferees: "To make a bold and synoptic approach to the discipline of public administration and . . . to measure the importance of public administration in the broad philosophic context."[1]

The lengthy conference report concludes: (1) Administrative agencies are policy makers. (2) The policy administration dichotomy is out of date. (3) It is difficult to define public administration and to mark its boundaries. (4) There is a big difference between public administration and business administration. (5) There is a sharp difference between public administration and the discipline of political science. (6) The theory of public administration, both normative and descriptive, was in the state of disarray. (7) The hierarchy was no longer an appropriate way to define or describe public organization. (8) Managerial and administrative concerns in public administration were being replaced by policy and political issues. (9) There should emerge some professional schools of public administration. (10) Public administration had not addressed itself in a significant way to pressing social problems such as the military-industrial complex, the labor movement, urban riots, etc. (11) The field had been too preoccupied with intellectual categories, semantics, definitions, and boundaries.[2]

There was sharp criticism of the conference, particularly by younger theorists, practitioners, and students. The numerous criticisms of the American Academy of Political and Social Science Conference on Public Administration included (1) avoiding the major issues of the time: urban race riots, poverty, the war in Vietnam, the ethical responsibilities of public officials; (2) a failure to be bold in suggesting positive new concepts or theories; (3) a preoccupation with ideas, concepts, and theories developed prior to 1960; (4) an insufficient interest in social and organizational change; (5) too much trust in expertise and organizational capabilities and too little questioning of bureaucratic ways; (6) not enough concern for limits on growth, organizational cutback, and decline; (7) not enough concern for citizens' demands and needs and the issues of responsiveness except by elected officials; (8) an overoptimistic view of what government and administration either can or should accomplish.

Dwight Waldo was impressed by the fact that the conferees were generally in their fifties and sixties, and he openly wondered why the public administrators and public administration professors of the next generation were absent. Thus was born the idea of a separate conference dealing with public administration—but limited to persons thirty-five years of age or younger. Such a conference was held, and a starkly different point of view and literature emerged. Three principal pieces of literature emerged from this conference and subsequent meetings: Frank Marini, *Toward a New Public Administration: The Minnowbrook Perspective*; Dwight Waldo, *Public Administration in a Time of Turbulence*; and H. George Frederickson, *Neighborhood Control in the 1970s*. Of the many themes in these books, some are dominant in all three. Frank Marini identified the major themes at the Minnowbrook Conference as relevance; postpositivism; adaption to a turbulent environment; new forms of organization; and client-focused organizations. All of these themes are developed in other parts of the new public administration literature, and they are developed more fully in this book.

Second, one of the more interesting aspects of the emergence of new public administration was the problem of personal responsibility. Dwight Waldo was the editor in chief of the major journal in the field, *Public Administration Review*, during this entire period. Frank Marini was the managing editor, and I was the research and reports editor. We were determined not to use the *Public Administration Review* as a vehicle for propagandizing or attempting to dominate the field with the views of those who identified themselves with the so-called new public administration. In fact, a conscious attempt was made during this period not to use the phrase "new public administration." This is probably the single most important reason why many have concluded that new public administration simply disappeared. What happened was the opposite—the *phrase* was generally dropped in the *Public Administration Review*, but the concepts and ideas associated with new public administration are very much a part of that journal as well as the general public administration literature through the decade of the 1970s.

Third, the dominant professional organization to which most persons in the field belong is the American Society for Public Administration. The 1970 annual conference of the

American Society for Public Administration was held in Philadelphia. At that meeting, a set of unauthorized panels, workshops, and meetings were held, under the label the "Unconvention." The "Unconvention" was organized to protest the program presented by the Conference Committee because that committee had not given sufficient attention to the critical issues of the time. By the last day of the conference, more persons were attending the meetings of the "Unconvention" than those of the formal conference.

It was also at the Philadelphia conference in 1970 that a slate of candidates was put forward for the presidency of the organization and for its National Council in opposition to those presented by the Nominating Committee. The challenging presidential candidate and council aspirants won the election. Consequently, many younger people and persons identified with the new public administration and the Unconvention took positions of responsibility in ASPA only to discover that the organization was in a serious fiscal crisis. That crisis was overcome, and the organization was made significantly more democratic and much more responsive. ASPA now takes positions on the great issues of the day. It has an open nominating and electoral process. It has an enviable record of electing women and minorities to office. It has grown, changed, and prospered and is in sound fiscal condition.

This book has been written with the benefit of hindsight. New public administration identified values and ethics as the critical issue for the 1970s. That appraisal turned out to be exactly correct. New public administration deals at some length with strategies and approaches to organizational decline and cutback. That forecast turned out to be exactly correct. And assessments of the era of limits and of no growth were made that were exactly correct. There are many other examples of relevant judgments that have influenced public administration throughout the 1970s and into the 1980s. And there were errors and poor guesses, particularly having to do with intractable poverty and the maldistribution of wealth, resources, and opportunity.

Dwight Waldo characterized new public administration as follows:

> Its adherents were centrally involved in change in the American Society for Public Administration designed to give it a more forward stance. The literature it has produced is widely read; its ideas and sentiments circulate in the public administration community, particularly academia. As its adherents both original and converts are largely on the young side and still to reach positions of maximum influence, it is likely to exert a continuing, if unpredictable, influence. In brief, it is unlikely to transform radically public administration short run but long run there is a possibility; and in any case it now is and will continue to be a yeasty addition to the entire complex of theories, techniques, and aspirations.[3]

If Waldo's assessment is accurate that new public administration has had an important impact on the field, then a thorough explanation of this subject is called for. That is the purpose of this book.

New Public Administration

1: Introduction

The problem is: how can we make government
competent and authoritative without destroying
the values of democratic participation and
responsibility?—Don K. Price, "1984 and Beyond:
Social Engineering or Political Values"

The national bicentennial in 1976 marked two important
birthdays for public administration. It was the ninetieth 90th
anniversary of the appearance of the first fully developed
essay on what was considered a "new" or at least a separately identified field—public administration. In that essay,
the young political scientist Woodrow Wilson wrote the now
famous words, "administration lies outside the proper
sphere of politics. Administrative questions are not political
questions; although politics sets the tasks for administration,
it should not be suffered to manipulate its offices."[1]
And it was exactly fifty years since the publication of
Leonard White's text, *Introduction to the Study of Public
Administration*, the first in the field.[2] White's book was, for
his time, an advanced and sophisticated attempt to marry
the science of government and the science of administration.
Whereas Wilson had argued that public administration is "a
field of business" and should be separate from "politics,"
White forty years later countered that public administration
can be effective only if it constitutes an integration of the
theory of government and the theory of administration.
As fields or professions go, public administration is young.
Its early impetus was very much connected with civil service
reform, the city manager movement, the "good government" movement, and the professionalization of the administrative apparatus of government. It was in this era that
"principles of administration" were developed and the first
academic programs in the field were established at American

universities. This was a heady era, during which the United States civil service was developed, an innovation adopted in many American states and municipalities. Formal systems of budgeting and purchasing were adopted, and other aspects of the science of management were applied to government affairs. Many of the early leaders in this reform movement also played out important political roles, most notably Theodore Roosevelt and Woodrow Wilson. Public administration was new, a response to a rapidly changing government.

The second "era" in public administration could be said to have begun with the Depression and the New Deal, followed by World War II. This era was characterized by the remarkably rapid growth of the government, particularly at the national level, the development of major American social programs, and ultimately the development of a huge defense program. At this time it became apparent that a large and centralized government can accomplish heroic tasks. Patterns were being developed and attitudes framed for the conduct of American government and the practices of public administration for the coming twenty years. This era also produced most of the major American scholars in public administration who were to dominate the scene from the 1940s into the 1970s.

The period that followed was characterized by rapid growth in the public service and by extensive suburbanization and urbanization. But it was also a period of great questioning of the purposes and premises of public administration. A broad variety of social programs and services were developed, a cold war machine was maintained, and the public service continued both to grow and to professionalize. It seemed as if such expansion could go on endlessly. But by the mid-1960s several crises were developing simultaneously. In many ways, these crises seemed in part to result from the excesses of an earlier time. In other ways, they seemed to be an expression of old and unanswered problems built into our society and our system of government. The urban crisis resulted from relentless suburbanization—governmentally supported. The racial crisis is closely connected, resulting in part from the serious ghettoization of American minorities in the central sections of our great cities. As the central cities have deteriorated, so have their public services. We continue to have unacceptable levels of unemployment, especially among minorities. And our welfare system is badly overloaded. The rapid depletion of our fuel resources results in an energy crisis, which comes hard on the heels of the environmental crisis. And, of course, there is health care, transportation, and on and on. All of these crises have affected public administration.

Three particular events or activities occurred between the mid-1960s and 1970s that indelibly marked the society and the government and, hence, public administration: the war in Vietnam, the urban riots and continued racial strife, and Watergate. These crises and events resulted in new government programs and changed ways of thinking about and practicing public administration.

Frederick C. Mosher and John C. Honey studied the characteristics and composition of the public service in the mid-1960s.[3] Their basic finding was that most public servants feel little or no identity with the field of public administration. Few have ever had a course and fewer still hold a degree in the subject. Public administration at the time seemed to have a rather narrow definition of its purposes, centering primarily on budgeting, personnel, and organization and management problems. Most public servants, it was found, identify with some or another professional field, such as education, community planning, law, public health, or engineering. Even many of those who would be expected to identify with public administration are more particularly interested in some subset of the field, such as finance, personnel, policy analysis, and the like. There was very little policy emphasis in public administration—very little discussion of defense policy, environmental policy, economic policy, urban policy. There was, at the time, much talk of public administration as everyone's "second profession." Education for public administration in the mid-1960s hardly sparkled. The early furor of the reformers had died. The American Society for Public Administration was beginning to struggle.

By the late 1970s, public administration had changed, both in its practice and its teaching. There are many indicators: the Intergovernmental Personnel Act; Title IX of the Higher Education Act; the Federal Executive Institute and the Federal Executive Seminars; the remarkable growth and vigor of education for public service; the President's Management Intern Program; the Harry S. Truman Foundation; the size and quality of ASPA; the development of the Consortium on Education for the Public Service; several HUD grants to public administration-related activities; a much heavier policy emphasis; a renewed concern for ethics and morality in government service; and the continued professionalization of the public service coupled with refinement of management methods at all levels of government.

Public administration is both changed and new. What, then, can be said of this field, or occupation, or profession, that is new? How can it be described? To what extent is it the culmination of the thinking and practices of those who have built the public service, and to what extent is modern public administration different than predicted or expected? Is it a creature as responsive to its times as it is to its lineage? The purpose of this book is to sketch the outlines of contemporary public administration and to set out my "best guesses" as to the likely characteristics and behavior of our field over the near-term future (say, ten to twenty years).

What Is New Public Administration?

To affix the label "new" to anything is risky business. The risk is doubled when newness is attributed to ideas, thoughts, concepts, paradigms, theories. Those who claim new thinking tend to regard previous thought as old or jejune or both. In response, the authors of previous thought are defensive and inclined to suggest that aside from having packaged earlier thinking in a new vocabulary there is little that is really new in so-called new thinking. Accept, therefore, this caveat: Parts of new public administration would be recognized by Plato, Hobbes, Machiavelli, Hamilton, and Jefferson as well as by many modern behavioral theorists. The newness is in the way the fabric is woven, not necessarily in the threads that are used. And the newness is in arguments as to the proper use of the fabric—however threadbare.

The threads of the public administration fabric are well known. Herbert Kaufman describes them simply as the pursuit of these basic values: representativeness, politically neutral competence, and executive leadership.[4] In different times, one or the other of these values receives the greatest emphasis. Representativeness was preeminent in the Jacksonian era. The eventual reaction was the reform movement emphasizing neutral competence and executive leadership. Now we are witnessing a revolt against these values accompanied by a search for new modes of representativeness.

Others have argued that changes in public administration resemble a zero-sum game between administrative efficiency and political responsiveness. Any increase in efficiency results a priori in a decrease in responsiveness. We are simply entering a period during which political responsiveness is to be purchased at a cost in administrative efficiency.

Both the trichotomous and dichotomous value models of public administration just described are correct as gross generalizations. But they suffer the weakness of gross generalizations: they fail to account for the wide, often rich, and sometimes subtle variation that rests within. Moreover, the generalization does not explain those parts of public administration that are beyond its sweep. Describing new public administration in some detail is a means by which these generalizations can be given substance.

Social Equity

Educators have as their basic objective, and most convenient rationale, expanding and transmitting knowledge. The police are enforcing the law. Public health agencies lengthen life by fighting disease. Firemen, sanitation men, welfare workers, diplomats, the military, and so forth, all are employed by public agencies. Each specialization or profession has its own substantive set of objectives and therefore its rationale.

What, then, is public administration? What are its objectives and its rationale?

The classic answer had always been the efficient, economical, and coordinated management of the services listed above. The focus has been on top-level management (city management as an example) or the basic auxiliary staff services (budgeting, organization and management, systems analysis, planning, personnel, purchasing). The rationale for public administration is almost always better (more efficient or economical) management. New public administration adds social equity to the classic objectives and rationale. Conventional or classic public administration seeks to answer either of these questions: (1) How can we offer more or better services with available resources (efficiency)? or (2) How can we maintain our level of services while spending less money (economy)? New public administration adds this question: Does this service enhance social equity?

Social equity is a phrase that comprehends an array of value preferences, organizational design preferences, and management style preferences. Social equity emphasizes equality in government services. Social equity emphasizes responsibility for decisions and program implementation for public managers. Social equity emphasizes change in public management. Social equity emphasizes responsiveness to the needs of citizens rather than the needs of public organizations. Social equity emphasizes an approach to the study of and education for public administration that is interdisciplinary, applied, problem solving in character, and sound theoretically.

Inequality

One of the basic concerns of new public administration is the equitable treatment of citizens. Social equity works from these value premises. Pluralistic government systematically discriminates in favor of established, stable bureaucracies and their specialized minority clientele (the Department of Agriculture and large farmers as an example) and against those minorities (farm laborers, both migrant and permanent, as an example) who lack political and economic resources. The continuation of widespread unemployment, poverty, disease, ignorance, and hopelessness in an era of economic growth is the result. This condition is morally reprehensible and if left unchanged constitutes a fundamental, if long-range, threat to the viability of this or any political system. Continued deprivation amid plenty breeds widespread militancy. Militancy is followed by repression, which is followed by greater militancy, and so forth. A public administration that fails to work for changes to try to redress the deprivation of minorities will likely eventually be used to repress those minorities.

For a variety of reasons—probably the most important being committee legislatures, seniority legislatures, entrenched bureaucracies, nondemocratized political-party procedures, inequitable revenue-raising capacity in the lesser governments of the federal system—the procedures of representative democracy presently operate in a way that either fails or only very gradually attempts to reverse systematic discrimination against disadvantaged minorities. Social equity, then, includes activities designed to enhance the political power and economic well-being of these minorities.

Value-Free Public Administration?

A fundamental commitment to social equity means that new public administration attempts to come to grips with Dwight Waldo's contention that the field has never satisfactorily accommodated the theoretical implications of involvement in "politics" and policy making.[5] The policy-administration dichotomy lacks an empirical warrant, for it is abundantly clear that administrators both execute and make policy. The policy-administration continuum is more accurate empirically but simply begs the theoretical question. New public administration attempts to answer it in this way: Administrators are not neutral. They should be committed to both good management and social equity as values, things to be achieved, or rationales.

Change

A fundamental commitment to social equity means that new public administration is anxiously engaged in change. Simply put, new public administration seeks to change those policies and structures that systematically inhibit social equity. This is not seeking change for change's sake nor is it advocating alterations in the relative roles of administrators, executives, legislators, or the courts in our basic constitutional forms. Educators, agriculturists, police, and the like can work for changes that enhance their objectives and resist those that threaten those objectives, all within the framework of our governmental system. New public administration works in the same way to seek the changes that would enhance its objectives—good management, efficiency, economy, and social equity.

A commitment to social equity not only involves the pursuit of change but attempts to find organizational and political forms that exhibit a capacity for continued flexibility or routinized change. Traditional bureaucracy has a demonstrated capacity for stability, indeed, ultrastability.[6] New public administration, in its search for changeable structures, tends therefore to experiment with or advocate modified bureaucratic organizational forms. Decentralization, devolution, termination, projects, contracts, evaluation, organization development, responsibility expansion, confrontation, and client involvement are all essentially counterbureaucratic notions that characterize new public administration. These concepts are designed to enhance the potential for change in the bureaucracy and to further policy changes that increase possibilities for social equity.

Other organizational tools such as programming-planning-budgeting systems, policy analysis, productivity measurement, zero-base budgeting, and reorganization, can be seen as enhancing change in the direction of social equity. They are almost always presented in terms of good management as a basic strategy, because it is unwise to advocate change frontally.[7] In point of fact, however, these tools can be used as basic devices for change. Both policy analysis and productivity measurement are fundamental to determining the quality and distribution of public costs and benefits. PPB and zero-base budgeting are useful tools for challenging the present patterns of public expenditures and planning public programs with some promise of accomplishing specified objectives. Reorganization is a basic tool for realigning organizational skills to best meet public needs. All three of these notions have only a surface neutrality or good-management character. Under the surface they are devices by which administrators and executives try to bring about change. It is no wonder they are so widely favored in public administration circles. And it should not be surprising that economists and political scientists in the "pluralist" camp regard devices such as PPB as fundamentally threatening to their conception of democratic government.[8] Although they are more subtle in terms of change, PPB, productivity measurement, and policy analysis belong to the same genre as more frontal change techniques such as organizational development, projects, contracts, decentralization, and the like. All enhance change, and change is basic to new public administration.

New public administration's commitment to social equity implies a strong administrative or executive government—what Alexander Hamilton called "energy in the executive." The policy-making powers of the administrative parts of government are increasingly recognized. In addition, a fundamentally new form of political access and representativeness is now occurring in the administration of government, and this access and representativeness may be as critical to major policy decisions as is legislative access or representativeness. New public administration seeks not only to carry out legislative mandates as efficiently and economically as possible, but both to influence and to execute policies that more generally improve the quality of life for all. Forthright policy advocacy on the part of the public servant is essential if administrative agencies are basic policy battlefields. Policy advocacy is as old as management. Where is the department head or bureau chief who does not try to improve the department budget, salary, facilities, benefits? And certainly no one would want a police chief, a school superintendent, or a secretary of defense who did not believe the function of that agency to be anything less than vital to the well-being of the polity. New public administration emphasizes the social purposes of the agency rather than well-being of the agency—recognizing, however, that both are important.

Classic public administration emphasizes developing and strengthening institutions that have been designed to deal with social problems. The public administration focus, however, has tended to drift from the problem to the institution. New public administration attempts to refocus on the problem and to consider alternative possible institutional approaches to confronting problems. The intractable character of such public problems as urban poverty, unemployment, and health care lead public administrators seriously to question the investment of ever more money and manpower in institutions that seem only to worsen the problems. They seek, therefore, either to modify these institutions or to develop new and more easily changed ones designed to achieve more proximate solutions. New public administration is concerned less with the Defense Department than with defense, less with civil service commissions than with the manpower needs of administrative agencies on the one hand and the employment needs of the society on the other, less with building institutions and more with designing alternate means of solving public problems. These alternatives will no doubt have some recognizable organizational characteristics, and they will need to be built and maintained, but they will seek to avoid becoming entrenched, nonresponsible bureaucracies that become greater public problems than the social situations they were originally designed to improve.

The movement from an emphasis on institution building and maintenance to an emphasis on social anomalies has an important analogue in the study of public administration. The last generation of students of public administration generally accept both Herbert Simon's logical positivism and his call for an empirically based organization theory. They focus on generic concepts such as decision, role, and group theory to develop a generalizable body of organization theory. The search is for commonalities of behavior in all organizational settings.[9] The organization and the people within it are the empirical referent. The product is usually description, not prescription, and if it is prescription it prescribes how to manage the organization better internally. The subject matter is first organization and second the type of organization—private, public, or voluntary. The two main bodies of theory emerging from this generation of work are decision theory and human relations theory. Both are regarded as behavioral and positivist. Both are at least as heavily influenced by sociology, social psychology, and economics as they are by political science.[10]

New public administration advocates could be best described as "postbehavioralists." Unlike his progenitor, the postbehavioralist emphasizes the public part of public administration. The postbehavioralist accepts the importance of understanding as scientifically as possible how and why organizations behave as they do, but he tends to be rather more interested in the impact of that organization on its clientele and vice versa. He or she is not antipositivist or antiscientific although probably less than sanguine about the applicability of the natural science model to social phenomena. He or she is not likely to use behavioralism as a rationale for simply trying to describe how public organizations behave. Nor is he or she inclined to use behavioralism as a façade for so-called neutrality, being more than a little skeptical of the objectivity of those who claim to be doing science. The postbehavioralist attempts to use scientific skills to aid analysis, experimentation, and evaluation of alternative policies and administrative modes. In sum, then, the postbehavioralist is less "generic" and more "public" than his forebear, less "descriptive" and more "prescriptive," less "institution oriented" and more "client-impact oriented," less "neutral" and more "normative," and, it is hoped, no less scientific.

Participation

New public administration's commitment to responsiveness and social equity implies participation. Some advocates of new public administration emphasize internal participation. The positive effects of the ability of public servants to be involved in and influence the policies that govern their work has been empirically demonstrated. Open and fully participative decision processes have long been canons of good management practice. Other advocates of new public administration emphasize citizen participation in the policy-making process. This view is most commonly found among those who practice or teach local government and work with the so-called street-level bureaucracies. Thus, citizen participation, neighborhood control, decentralization, and democratic work environments are standard themes in new public administration.

This has been a brief and admittedly surface description of new public administration from the perspective of one analyst. If the description is even partially accurate, it is patently clear that fundamental changes are occurring in public administration that have salient implications for both its study and practice as well as for the general conduct of government.

2: New Public Administration in Context

The primary instrument of our success in this century
has been neither our military prowess nor our wealth,
but our most successful social invention: the modern
organization. Americans have moved into this last
quarter of the twentieth century with only the slightest
awareness that the modern organization, with its accouterments
of power and control, has become the dominant force in
our lives, shaping and changing American values and the
American people to suit its requirements. Modern organizations
have influenced us so profoundly, but so quietly that we
are scarcely aware that they are our major agencies for
social control. We take them for granted in much the same
way we accept television commercials, the "two minute warning,"
and Muzak.—William G. Scott and David K. Hart,
Organizational America

New public administration emerged in the late 1960s and
early 1970s as a response to several stimuli, most notably the
war in Vietnam, continuing racial unrest, continuing dissat-
isfaction with the intellectual basis of public administration,
and the general shifting going on in the social science
disciplines. The three major collections of essays generally
identified with new public administration (Frank Marini's
Toward a New Public Administration, Dwight Waldo's *Public Administration in a Time of Turbulence*, and George
Frederickson's *Neighborhood Control in the 1970s*) serve to
illustrate that there is not *a* new public administration or *the*
new public administration.[1] There is, rather, a rich variety of
interpretations of what is going on in the social sciences and
how that applies to public problems. There is a wide array of
values associated with new public administration, and these
values are not always consistent. Therefore, I strongly resist
the notion that there must be a single, agreed-upon new
public administration with an attendant model that is a

complete negation of past theory and norms in the field. This is, then, an argument that what is new in new public administration flows directly from the values that guided traditional public administration. And new public administration proceeds logically from the aggregation of new knowledge in the social sciences and the focusing of those sciences on public problems. If this is the case, then new public administration has a rich and significant lineage. A description of this lineage might serve to put new public administration in context and clarify its objectives.

Political Science

Any consideration of public administration should begin with political science. Clearly, political science is the mother discipline, and almost all of the early American public administration theorists were political scientists (Woodrow Wilson, W. W. Willoughby, Frank Goodnow, Leonard White, Paul Appleby, John Pfiffner). Political science, and particularly political theory, has traditionally been the locus of the most complete consideration of the normative and philosophical thought that now appears central to public administration. But public administration has always been both more than and less than political science.

In the university, public administration is more than political science in that those who either study or prepare for public administration are more likely to study social psychology and economics than political science.[2] The drift of public administration away from political science is seen in the emergence of schools of public affairs and public policy.[3] We further sense the separation of political science from public administration by the occasional discovery on the part of political scientists that the mother discipline has kept this particular child undernourished and in the corner. But it is the concentration by public administration scholars on theories, constructs, and models from the other social sciences that really marks the importance of the public administration drift from political science. In the government agency, public administration has always been more than political science because the agency is usually staffed by specialists from other disciplines. Few of these specialists have any educational background in public administration, let alone political science. And public administration has always been less than political science, a child of the mother discipline with an uneasy relationship with its mother and a hearty and fruitful search for its "fathers" in the other disciplines.

Most political scientists readily acknowledge the size and power of the bureaucracy. Frances E. Rourke argues that

> a variety of circumstances in modern life, as, for example, the growing weight of expert knowledge in policy formation, continue to push bureaucracy toward a position of pre-eminence in the governing process . . . this bureaucratic power rests partly on the extraordinary capacities of public agencies as sources of expertise, but partly also on the fact that administrative agencies have become major centers for the mobilization of political energy and support. As a result, bureaucratic politics rather than party politics has become the dominant theater of decision in the modern state.[4]

Therefore, it would be logical to assume that bureaucracy would be an important subject to those who study government. Yet the great numbers of men and women employed to carry out government programs—the bureaucrats—are perhaps the least studied actors in American government, at least by political scientists. A recent survey of the research and publishing habits of political scientists shows that only 7 percent of the articles published in political science deal with bureaucracy and the executive branch of government. To understand modern public administration one must go well beyond political science.

Another way of making the same point is to assert that public administration is not a social science or a discipline but is an application of social science (and other science) to public problems. It is a subject matter, a profession, and a field. Public administration bridges the disciplines and, therefore, takes relevant parts of the disciplines and applies them to public problems. This is not to say that public administration is not academically or scientifically creative. In fact, it is the bridging and applying function that gives public administration its most exciting intellectual thrusts. The potential for a subject such as public administration to make a scientific breakthrough is at least as great as the potential of the disciplines.

The publication of Thomas Kuhn's *Structure of Scientific Revolutions* has caused a scurrying to find the paradigm in every field in social sciences.[5] It is intriguing that political scientists not long identified with public administration would take the view that the field is theoretically barren. There are, in fact, five major models in modern public administration, each with its major theorists, empirical referents, postulates, hypotheses, and norms. But most of the research and literature upon which these models are based are not found in political science. The theoretical richness of public administration is noticeably greater than in most other fields of political science primarily because public administration is a "borrowing" field. But the explication and comparison of these theories or models is customarily in the fields from which it borrows: sociology, social psychology, economics, and other disciplines.

For purposes of explication, five "models" of public administration are used to organize and categorize public administration. These models are set out in terms of theory, taking theory to mean positive or empirically based knowledge. The second purpose of this chapter is to discuss and compare these models in terms of values, using values to move beyond empirically supported arguments to arguments found in contemporary political philosophy as to what constitutes good government, ethical behavior, and sound moral reasoning. Values (norms) are, therefore, taken to mean the normative suppositions within or underlying the models being discussed and the process of moral reasoning in support of the models. After setting out these models, new public administration is described in value terms, and the lineage between new public administration and the five models is sketched.

Five Models in Public Administration

The five basic models in contemporary public administration are labeled here the classic bureaucratic model, the neobureaucratic model, the institutional model, the human relations model, and the public choice model (see Table 1). The labels are not especially important but are increasingly in common usage, except possibly in the case of what I designate the neobureaucratic model. The theorists put into that category may identify with one of the other categories or will resist being categorized at all. The grouping of theorists is less important (although professionally risky) than the integrity of the five models. In the description of the models and their theoretical and normative characteristics, it will become apparent that although there is an attempt to illustrate the integrity within each model, there are theorists who are really hybrids. Both the research literature and the synthesis literature in each of these models are sufficiently well developed so that it will not be necessary to review that literature. It is assumed that the reader is familiar with the literature and the major theorists. The consideration of theory and values in these models is done with these caveats.

The Classic Bureaucratic Model

If there is a dominant reality in the practice of American public administration it is the persistence and endurance of the classic bureaucratic model. The bureaucratic model has two basic components, the first being the structure or design of an organization, the second being the means by which persons and work are managed within the organizational design. Max Weber's ideal type is the general beginning point for any understanding of the structural aspects of

Table 1. Five Public Administration Models

Theories and Theorists	Empirical Focus (Unit of Analysis)	Characteristics	Values to be Maximized
Classic Bureaucratic Model	The organization	Structure, hierarchy, control, authority, policy-administration dichotomy, chain of command, unity of command, span of control, merit appointment, centralization	Efficiency Economy Effectiveness
Taylor	The production group		
Wilson	The government agency		
Weber	The bureau		
Gulick, Urwick	The work group		
Neobureaucratic Model	The decision	Logical-positivist, operations research, systems analysis, cybernetics, management science, productivity	Rationality Efficiency Economy Productivity
Simon, Cyert			
March, Gore			
Institutional Model	The decision (rational)	Empirical, positivist, bureaucracy is an expression of culture, patterns of bureaucratic behavior focusing on survival, competition, technology, rationality, incrementalism, power	Science "Neutral analysis of organizational behavior" Incrementalism Pluralism Criticism
Lindbloom	The decision (incremental)		
J. Thompson	Organizational behavior (open systems)		
Crozier	Organizational behavior		
Downs	Individual and organizational behavior		
Mosher	Bureaus and professions		
Etzioni	Comparative organizational behavior (power)		

Blau	Organization behavior (ex-changes)		
Riggs	Organization and culture		
V. Thompson	Organizational behavior		
Selznick	Organizational behavior (organis-mic)		
Human Relations Model	The individual and the work group	Interpersonal and inter-group relations, commu-nications, sanctions, motivation, change, training, shared au-thority, procedural cor-rectness, consensus	Worker satisfaction
McGregor	Supervisor/worker relations		Personal growth
Likert	Supervisor/worker performance		Individual dignity
Bennis	Behavior change		
Argyris	Behavior change		
Public Choice Model	Organization/client relations and public goods distribution	Antibureaucratic, appli-cation of economic logic to problems of public service distribution, highly analytic, market analogues, contracts, smallness, decentraliza-tion, bargaining	Citizen options or choices
Ostrom	Decentralized overlapping struc-tures		Equal access to services
			Competition
Buchanan, Tullock	Public sector as market		
Olson	Client group size and public ser-vice distribution		
Mitchell	Distribution		
Frohlich, Oppen-heimer, Young	Leadership and goods distribu-tion		
Niskanan	Performance contracting		

bureaucracy. In the national government, hierarchy and bureaucracy are seen in the preoccupation with organization charts and the fitting of persons into those organization charts (and even having the charts officially signed by "authorities") along with the elaborate development of job descriptions, personnel classifications, and pay scales. Weber also considered in his description of hierarchy some of the patterns of behavior exhibited by those in scalar organizations, such as the tendency to keep elaborate records, to attempt symmetry in command, and the like.

In its managerial and micro aspects, the classic bureaucratic model begins with Frederick Winslow Taylor's scientific management and can be traced from his initial notions of understanding productivity via time and motion studies to modern-day attempts to measure productivity.[6] In the classic bureaucratic model, structure and management are closely linked. The clearest expression of that linkage is seen in the literature on reorganization. When management or productivity are in trouble, resorting to reorganization, to redesigning the machine, to restructuring, is standard bureaucratic practice.[7] Hierarchy and managerial control are still the existential facts of American public organization. Indeed, Herbert Wilcox makes compelling arguments based on his research with children that management control and hierachy are so much a part of Western and particularly American culture that it is very difficult for products of this culture to imagine complex organization structured in other than scalar ways or managed other than through traditional means of control.[8]

The problem with the classic bureaucratic model was that both practitioners and scholars attempted to make a strict applied science of the design of organization or of the management of organization. The assumption that there was one best way to manage or design a particular organization was obviously faulty. Many of the early attempts to make a science of organizational structure and management were properly criticized by Herbert Simon in his designation of these scientific principles as "proverbs." But to suggest that there is or cannot be a strict science of organization design or management is not to suggest that structure and management are unimportant. No one would sensibly suggest the random arrangement of workers, nor would they assume that a product would emerge from a complex organization if there were no means by which workers were caused to arrange themselves in a cooperative and productive fashion. The problem, then, has not been one of developing a science of organizational design or a science of management; the problem is one of creating designs that are compatible with organizational objectives suitable to workers' needs and desired by "the public."

The values articulated by those who developed the classic bureaucratic model are as valid and compelling now as they were fifty years ago. To carry out a public function as fully as possible for the money available (a strict definition of efficiency) is, I would argue, fundamental to any theory or model in public administration. Similarly, carrying out public programs for the least possible money (a strict definition of economy) is equally as basic to any notion of an effective public administration. That an organization should be as productive as possible, that is, providing a quantity and quality of service that matches the expressed needs of a collectivity, is likewise a basic value in public administration.

The values of efficiency and economy are, therefore, a part of new public administration. The problem, then, is not with the values that were to maximize in the classic bureaucratic models. The problem was in the manner in which it was assumed that efficiency, economy, and productivity could be achieved. Hierarchy, managerial control, authority, and centralization are not as logically linked to the achievement of these values as the early bureaucratic theorists believed. Indeed, much of the work of the organization theorists, who are categorized here as neobureaucratic or human relationists, is about the business of demonstrating that effectiveness, economy, and efficiency are products of relaxed controls, loosened hierarchies, and the breaking down of authoritarian leadership styles.

The Neobureaucratic Model

The neobueaucratic model is one of the products of the behavioral era in social science. The values to be maximized in this model are generally similar to those of the bureaucratic model; therefore the designation "neobureaucratic." In most other respects the models differ. The bureaucratic model emphasizes structure, control, and the principles of administration, with the unit of analysis usually being the work group, the agency, the department, or whole governments. The values to be achieved are effectiveness, efficiency, or economy. In the neobureaucratic model, the decision is the more common unit of analysis, with the process of decision making being the central focus. The pattern of reasoning is "rational"; that is, decisions are made to achieve as much of a given goal as possible. Modern "management science," systems analysis, and operations research are built on the early writings of Herbert Simon, James March, and Richard Cyert.[9] These theorists enriched their work with a deep understanding of formal and informal patterns of organizational control, the limits of rationality, and the like, but the basic modern versions of the neobureaucratic school have stayed with the original means-end logic growing out of logical positivism. The close similarities between means-end analysis of the neobureaucratic model and the policy-administration dichotomy of the bureaucratic model are obvious. The objectives of operations research, systems analysis, policy analysis, and management sciences are essentially the same as those of the bureaucratic theorists. Their work, however, is very sophisticated and contributes substantially to the attainment of efficiency, economy, and productivity.

There could be no better indications of the profound validity of the values that motivated those who designed or chronicled the classic bureaucratic model than can be seen in modern public administration under new banners and rubrics. It is essentially these same values that are being pursued with a marvelous numerical precision in the measurement of productivity, the subject of a recent symposium in the *Public Administration Review*.[10] The reading of that symposium indicates clearly that contemporary public administration is really not very different in attempting to achieve productivity by methods of measurements rather than by methods of structure and management. To be sure, contemporary approaches are much more scientific and analytically sophisticated, but they are still in pursuit of the values underlying the classic bureaucratic paradigm. Modern approaches to policy analysis do enable the administrator or the academic to assess the consequences or results of the operation of public programs more effectively than in the past. But the modern policy analysts and productivity measurers may have as weak a link in their logic as there was in the classic bureaucratic paradigm. If it is erroneous to assume that hierarchy, centralization, and managerial command will achieve efficiency, economy, and productivity, it is probably also erroneous to assume that policy analysis will achieve those objectives. Furthermore, it is probably erroneous to assume that either approach is necessarily the friend of democratic or popular control of government. At the same time, it is equally clear that the underlying values of rational decisions to achieve efficiency, economy, and effectiveness are, and always will be, central to any normative dialogue in public administration, and they are certainly central to new public administration. The questions, however, are two: how to achieve these values, and do these values conflict absolutely with other values that should be central to public administration?

The Institutional Model

The institutional model[11] is a product of the work of many social scientists in the 1940s, 1950s, and 1960s. In its basic manifestation it is more methodologically rigorous than was the work of those who initially described bureaucracy; therefore, its findings will have a stronger empirical warrant. The institutional model is the manifestation of the behavioral era, particularly in sociology and political science. An earlier and empirically rich version of this model can be found in the studies produced by the Inter-University Case Program.

The concern of the institutional theorist is less with how to design efficient, effective, or productive organizations and more with how to analyze and understand existing bureaucracies. These scholars are generally "positivist" in their perspective, searching for order in complex organizations or for discernible patterns of bureaucratic behavior. Public administration scholars categorized as institutional seem rather less interested in how to make government more efficient, economic, or productive than they are in simply finding out how complex organizations behave.

Within this category fall works such as James Thompson's remarkable synthesis of organizational behavior, one of the more complete models in modern social science.[12] Frederick Mosher's analysis and synthesis of the behavior or particular public bureaucratic professional groupings is both empirically and logically rich.[13] Amitai Etzioni's comparative analysis of complex organization is equally as complete an integration of the behavioral characteristics of bureaucracy.[14] The "scientists" of the behavioral era have significantly advanced the systematic understanding of bureaucratic behavior. Still there is no agreed-upon model or paradigm, but rather a body of knowledge generally going under the label "organization theory." Public administration scholars are both systematic users of and contributors to organization theory.

If organization theory and the institutional model have been as well developed as is claimed here, what are the normative foundations on which this body of knowledge rests?

As is their custom, behavioral scholars simply skirt the normative questions, making the claim that they are in the business of describing organization, not prescribing answers. Yet there are strong normative currents in the institutional model. One of these currents can be characterized as the school of concerned scholars who have analyzed bureaucracy and discovered it to be powerful, resistant to change, seemingly beyond legislative or executive controls, tending to isolate and seal off its technology and guarantee its sources of revenue, and tending to concern itself primarily with survival. After having discerned these behavioral patterns, the scholar either observes that bureaucracy is bad and we ought to figure out ways to control it or that this is just a natural phenomenon and the price a complex and advanced society must pay if it wishes government to provide services.

One of the few detailed attempts to defend the values of the institutional model is done by Charles Lindbloom, who argues that rationality is not only unlikely, it is also undesirable. In his *The Intelligence of Democracy: Decision-Making through Mutual Adjustment*, he argues that bureaucracies make decisions in incremental ways, that these are decision bargains and compromises (really the bargains and compromises of interest group elites), and that they move government gradually toward vague objectives.[15] Further, and most important, this is really the way democratic government ought to work. It is only through incremental decision making that the expertise and skills of the bureaucracy can be integrated with the policy preferences and political biases of elected officials. Those opposed to the incremental view claim it to be nothing more than an elaborate apology for the way an ineffective government system now operates. In the guise of "describing democracy," they reify and justify the weaknesses in democratic systems. In the name of empiricism, they conclude either, "That's how things are in complex organizations and there really isn't much which can be done about it," or, "That's how things are in complex organizations and that's probably how they should be."

The Human Relations Model

The human relations model is in many ways a reaction to the classic bureaucratic and the neobureaucratic models. The emphasis in bureaucratic theory on control, structure, efficiency, economy, and rationality virtually invited the development of the human relations movement. Traced to the Hawthorn experiment and to the works of Elton Mayo and his colleagues, the human relations movement has evolved to a highly empirical and strongly researched body of theory in which social psychologists tend to have been the major theorists. Probably the two major works to influence students of public administration have been Rensis Likert's *The Human Organization: Its Management and Value* and Daniel Katz and Robert Kahn's *The Social Psychology of Organizations.*[16]

The human relations model has its applied manifestations principally in group dynamics, sensitivity training, and organizational development. The emphasis in these training movements clearly reflects the values underlying the human relations model: worker and client participation in decision making, reduction in status differentiations, reduction in interpersonal competition, and emphasis on openness, honesty, self-actualization, and general worker satisfaction. The classic bureaucratic and the neobureaucratic models (with the possible exception of the rational decision theorists) clearly are fair empirical representations of public organizations. There is some considerable question, however, as to the impact of the human relations model on government administration. If there has been an impact, it has been slow and slight. This is not to suggest that the empirical findings of human relations theorists are inaccurate; the point is that these findings are based more on experiments and tests than on observations of ongoing complex organizations. Nor is it to suggest that the values on which the human relations movement is based are bogus. It does suggest that these values may be in competition with the values on which the classic and neobureaucratic models are based. For example, managerial control and shared authority may conflict, as will efficiency and procedural correctness. Still, the human relations school has provided compelling evidence that under certain conditions shared authority and worker satisfaction are positively correlated with productivity.

The best available description of the clash in values between these models has been done by David K. Hart and
William G. Scott.[17] They first describe the remarkable similarities between the classic political theorist Thomas Hobbes
and Frederick Taylor, the father of scientific management:
(1) Man's nature is essentially evil, slothful, and indolent.
(2) This being the case, there must be controls to keep evil
men from destroying each other. (3) Preferably, these controls are centralized and autocratic. (4) Although autocratic
controls on society (Hobbes) or on the organization (Taylor)
result in some loss of liberty, they also result in material
advantages, efficiency, and predictability.

Scott and Hart then describe the similarities between the
political philosophy of Jean Jacques Rousseau and Douglas
McGregor: (1) Men are inherently good, whereas organizations or governments can be evil. (2) Men must overcome
their institutions by a new consciousness, the release of
emotional strength, and the development of new structures
that permit openness, honesty, and authenticity—human
relations. (3) New structures are based on a general will or a
consensus, and those not conforming must be "trained" to
be "free."

Most modern human relations theorists are inclined toward the norms of Rousseau and McGregor, but these
norms are not the dominant reality in complex public organizations. Hobbes and Taylor seem to be carrying the day, but
the training activities of the human relations adherents may
be having some impact.

The Public Choice Model

The modern version of political economics is now customarily referred to as either "nonmarket economics" or the
"public choice" approach. This body of knowledge is rich in
tradition and intellectual rigor, but somewhat light in empirical evidence. Nevertheless, the public choice theorists
are having and will continue to have an important influence
on American public administration. Vincent Ostrom has

recently completed what is essentially a tying together of public choice logic, public administration history and theory, and political philosophy. In his book *The Intellectual Crisis in American Public Administration*, he compares the perspective on public administration developed by Woodrow Wilson, which he labels bureaucratic theory, with the perspectives of the public choice theorist, which he labels a "paradigm of democratic administration."[18] The Wilsonian perspective is, in Ostrom's judgment, a sharp departure from the Hamiltonian-Madisonian perspective on the nature of government. Both, however, trace more directly to the political philosophy of Hobbes. The Wilsonian, or bureaucratic, paradigm has the following components: there will always be a dominant center of power in any system of government; a society will be controlled by that single center of power, and the more power is unified and directed from a single center the more responsible it will become; the field of politics sets the task for administration, but the field of administration lies outside the proper sphere of politics; perfection in the hierarchial ordering of a professionally trained public service provides the structural conditions necessary for "good" administration; and perfection of "good" administration as above defined is a necessary condition for modernity in human civilization and for the advancement of human welfare.[19]

By contrast, the Ostrom interpretation of public choice perspectives, which he bases on the *Federalist*, or Hamilton and Madison, has the following features. The provision of public goods and services depends upon decisions taken by diverse sets of decision makers, and the political feasibility of each collective enterprise depends upon a favorable course of decisions in all essential decision structures over time. Public administration lies within the domain of politics. A variety of different organizational arrangements can be used to provide different public goods and services. Such organizations can be coordinated through various multiorganizational arrangements, including trading and contracting to mutual advantage, competitive rivalry, adjudication, and the power of command in limited hierarchies. Perfection in the hierarchial ordering of a professionally trained public service accountable to a single center of power will reduce the capability of a large administrative system to respond to diverse preferences among citizens for many different public goods and services and to cope with diverse environmental conditions. Fragmentation of authority among diverse decision centers with multiple veto capabilities within any one jurisdiction and the development of multiple, overlapping jurisdictions of widely different scales are necessary conditions for maintaining a stable political order that can advance human welfare under rapidly changing conditions.[20]

The Ostrom interpretation of the public choice approach may not be universally accepted by public choice theorists, but it is certainly the most theoretically developed argument. The values espoused by public choice theorists are difficult to fault. Citizen choice in services is compelling and can be achieved by moving to the suburban city that has the array of services wanted. But not all citizens have this choice. Competition among jurisdictions or agencies is also enticing, because competition may "tone up" the quality of services generally. But can we afford competition, and if so how much? If competition enhances efficiency and economy, does it enhance these values for everyone? Have market model applications in the private sector resulted in a wide range of real consumer choices and a high level of organizational productivity? Has the development of collective unionization in the private sector reduced the range of citizen choices and the level of productivity and would the same thing happen in the public sector as unions grow in power?

At the beginning of this chapter, I suggested that the values that guided traditional public administration—efficiency, economy, productivity, rationality—will have a heavy influence on new public administration. The classic, neobureaucratic, and institutional models of public administration emphasize these values and their characteristics. But the human relations and public choice models are departures because they emphasize the values of worker satisfaction, personal growth, individual dignity, and citizens' choice. In the next chapter, I integrate these values with those associated with social equity and set out a model for new public administration.

3: Social Equity and Public Administration

Man's capacity for justice
makes democracy possible, but
man's inclination to injustice
makes democracy necessary.
—Reinhold Niebuhr

It is popular to believe that there will be a wilting away of old models in public administration and the emergence of a totally new model. This pattern of theory and model evolution (and devolution) may be common in the life, physical, or natural sciences, as Thomas Kuhn suggests, but I am of the view that it is not common in the social sciences. My reasons are fairly simple and trace directly to the questions of linkage between theory and value. Public administration is, in many ways, the vehicle for implementing the values or preferences of individuals, groups, social classes, or whole societies. These values are ongoing or enduring, but they also are often competitive. At any point in time, one set of values may be dominant and have a lock on the practice of public administration, as I would contend the classic and neobureaucratic models now do. Therefore, efficiency, economy, productivity, and centralization are dominant norms, and bureaucratic behavior, as well as bureaucratic theory, reflect this domination.

If one can accept these arguments, then a concept of new public administration would have to begin with the argument that a different (and certainly not new) set of values should predominate. These values would be carried out by organizations that are humanistic, decentralized, democratic and that distribute public services equitably. New public administration, therefore, would be the attempt to organize, describe, design, or make operative organizations that further these norms. This clearly is a markedly less ambitious interpretation of the objectives of new public administration than many who identify with the field would accept. For example, it is standard practice to call for the "radical reconstruction of public administration" or for the development of a "new paradigm that reorients man."

These are catchy notions and often receive unwarranted attention in the academy, where premiums are paid for the freshness of an idea or for being on the "cutting edge" of "mind-breaking" positions.[1] The critical point is that most of these views are far too utopian to be feasible, or so abstract as to be nonoperational. All this is understandable, given the extent to which one takes seriously the label "new." If new public administration scholars or practitioners worried less about whether an idea is old or new and worried more about the extent to which the idea can be operationalized, then it is possible to develop a truly new public administration. In a very real sense, this is the most radical version of modern public administration because it identifies dominant values and seeks governmental means by which these values can be effectuated.

What, then, can be made of new public administration, both theoretically and normatively? First, new public administration must reject the notion that administrators are value-neutral or administrative theories are value-neutral models. Second, it must be recognized that the values listed on Table 1 in Chapter 2 are legitimate, although often in conflict. If they are in conflict, which values should dominate, given the present American political and administrative situation? And, perhaps more important, which political and administrative adjustments can further the pursuit of these values? Table 2 presents a list of values that seem to be a "constellation" of norms or sets of preferences that characterize what seems to concern contemporary public administration. This constellation of values is not at this point a model, but is, rather, the blending of models and values that seem at present to be the most compelling in our political and administrative lives. Not only are they compelling matters in a vague, normative sense, but they also have strong empirical support in modern social science, as well as an excellent basis in contemporary American political philosophy.

For example, an examination of modern social psychology, and particularly as that field bears on administrative behavior and complex organizations, makes it increasingly clear that nonauthoritarian forms of administration correlate with increases in worker morale, satisfaction, and productivity. This aspect of new public administration is then, little more than an extension of the human relations model.

There is further evidence that when citizens are offered an array of choices with respect to preferred public services, they select those services that *they* interpret as more responsive to their general needs, which is to say that the broadening of citizen choice equates with the responsiveness of bureaucracies.[2] Again, this flows logically from the public choice model. There is interesting research that indicates that citizen participation and neighborhood control do result in breaking down the dominance of managerial definitions of services that citizens need. Citizen participation and neighborhood control appear to result in a pattern of compromise and adjustment whereby managerial definitions of client needs are adjusted to citizen definitions of their needs.[3] These examples are particularly evident in the field of education, a field in which citizen participation, neighborhood control, and a general pattern of decentralization are clearly under way. It is also evident from some of this research that there are tradeoffs between the values upon which public administration is built. For example, neighborhood control and citizen participation in school decision making probably do result in some diminution in economy and efficiency. This decline in economy and efficiency, however, is offset by the increase in "responsiveness"; the citizens of a particular neighborhood are willing to forego some efficiency, as that term might be defined managerially, for a pattern of services that *they* prefer, even though that pattern of services may, from a classic public administration point of view, be inefficient. This serves to illustrate that a group of citizens might define a public service as effective in ways that are at rather distinct odds with either managerial or majority rule electoral officials' definitions of effectiveness.

If bureaucratic responsiveness, worker and citizen participation in decision making, social equity, citizen choice, and administrative responsibility for program effectiveness are the constellation of values to be maximized in modern public administration, what are the structural and managerial means by which these values can be achieved? Table 2 is an attempt to array the alternative means by which it is assumed these values are achieved. This is not to make a set of absolute causal assertions—such as decentralization will bring about responsiveness—it is simply to suggest probabilities, such as, the likelihood of bureaucratic responsiveness occurring seems greater under conditions of political and administrative decentralization. Table 2, then, is an attempt to summarize both the empirical literature (to include case studies and other nonquantitative forms of analysis), and some of the folklore of public administration.

Clearly, the most interesting developments in modern public administration are not empirical but are philosophical, normative, and speculative. Most of these are grouped here under the phrase "social equity." In public administration, the phrase "social equity" has emerged as a shorthand way of referring to the concerns and opinions of those who are challenging contemporary theory and practice. As yet, the phrase social equity, however, has little substance or precision. Much of the remainder of this chapter will describe, in a summary way, social equity as a positive expression of modern views in public administration. I shall not deal here with the traditional questions of ethics and responsibility in government. In the extent to which we deal with questions of ethics and responsibility in government, it will be from the perspective of social equity and new administration. This should not be regarded as a detailed consideration of ethics or morality in public administration. It is designed, rather, to posit a different approach both to theory building in public administration and to the practice of public administration.

Table 2. Values, Structure, and Management in Social Equity

Values to be Maximized	Structural Means of Achievement	Managerial Means of Achievement
Responsiveness	Decentralization (political and administrative) Contracting Neighborhood control over street-level bureaucracies	Routine client interaction with employees and managers Managerial definition of democracy, including more than responsiveness to elected officials, but also to interest groups and disorganized minorities Training
Worker and citizen participation in decision making	Neighborhood councils with power Overlapping work groups Worker involvement in decision processes	Acceptance of an ethic that insists on the right of workers and citizens to participate in those decision processes that affect their lives directly Training in organizational development
Social equity	Areawide revenue systems with local distribution systems Public service outputs and outcomes made equal by social class	Professional codes of ethics spelling out equity The managerial commitment to the principle that majority rule does not overturn minority rights to equal public services
Citizen choice	Devising alternative forms of services so as to broaden choice Overlap Contracting	Reduction of managerial monopoly over a particular service, such as health care or education
Administrative responsibility for program effectiveness	Decentralization Delegation Performance targets	Measuring performance, not only on general organizational standards, but also by social class Measuring performance for whom?

The problem of equity is as old as government. Dwight Waldo points out that "much governmental action in the United States has not been simply discriminatory but massively and harshly so. Much governmental action has also, however, been directed toward achieving equality; paradoxically, action to assure assimilation and uniformity also has sometimes been insensitive and coercive." "Equality," he concludes, "is central to the understanding of much recent and contemporary public administration."[4] It has been seriously suggested that social equity be a standard by which public administrators, both in the bureau and the academy, assess and evaluate their behavior and decisions. Social equity, then, would be a criterion for effectiveness in public administration in the same way that efficiency, economy, productivity, and other criteria are used. The rationale and defense of this criterion are spelled out in some detail here.

Whenever an ethic or standard for behavior is described, it is essential to provide an accompanying caveat. In the present case, the social equity point of view will need to be buffered by a recognition first that there is a high ethical content in most significant public decisions; public problems do not succumb simply to factual analysis. This being the case, if the public servant is to be an interpreter of events and an influencer, if not a maker of decisions, what, then, should be included in the standards of ethical behavior that guide the public servant? Surely the standards of ethics and morality that are applicable and sufficient to a citizen in private or in social relationships are not adequate for the public decisions of an administrator. And it is now increasingly clear that the decision problems faced by these administrators are seldom black or white in relation to their ethical content and consequences. There often is really no "one best way," but rather a decision should be made that maximizes such results as are attainable given the resources available and minimizes negative side effects. And finally, one must accept the proposition that politics and administrative organizations are themselves the best protectors of administrative morality provided that they are open, public, and participatory. Within this context, then, we pursue the development of a social equity ethic for public administration.

Theory and Definition

In the first chapter of this volume, I stated that conventional and classic public administration seeks to answer either of these questions: (1) How can we offer more or better services with available resources (efficiency)? or (2) How can we maintain our level of services while spending less money (economy)? A new public administration adds this question: Does this service enhance social equity?

To say that a service may be well managed and that a service may be efficient and economical, still begs these questions: Well managed for whom? Efficient for whom? Economical for whom? We have generally assumed in public administration a convenient oneness with the public. We have not focused our attention or concern to the issue of variations in social and economic conditions. It is of great convenience, both theoretically and practically, to assume that citizen A is the same as citizen B and that they both receive public services in equal measure. This assumption may be convenient, but it is obviously both illogical and empirically inaccurate. We see around us wealth and poverty, employment and unemployment, health and disease, knowledge and ignorance, hope and hopelessness. Modern public administration cannot assume these conditions away. Certainly pluralistic governments (practicing majority rule, coupled with powerful minorities with special forms of access) systematically discriminate in favor of established, stable bureaucracies and their specialized clientele—and against those minorities who lack political and economic resources. Thus widespread and deep inequity are perpetuated. The long-range continuation of widespread and deep inequities poses a threat to the continued existence of this or any political system. Continued deprivation amid plenty breeds hopelessness and her companions, anger and militancy. A public administration that fails to work for changes that try to address this deprivation will likely eventually be used to oppress the deprived.

What new public administration is striving for, then, is equity.

Black's Law Dictionary defines equity in its broadest and most general signification:

> [Equity] denotes the spirit and the habit of fairness and justness and right dealing which would regulate the inter-course of men with men,—the rule of doing to all others, as we desire them to do to us; or, as it is expressed by Justinian, "to live honestly, to harm nobody, to render every man his due." . . . It is therefore, the synonym of natural right or justice. But in this sense its obligation is ethical rather than jural, and its discussion belongs to the sphere of morals. It is grounded in the precepts of the conscience not in any sanction of positive law.[5]

Equity, then, is an issue that we will find to be a question of ethics. We will also find it to be a question of law.

The foremost theorist presently supporting a concept of equity in government is John Rawls. In his book *A Theory of Justice*, he sets out a splendid framework for a fundamental equity ethic. When speaking of our government institutions, Rawls states: "For us the primary subject of justice is the basic structure of society, or more exactly, the way in which the major social institutions distribute fundamental rights and duties and determine the division of advantages from social cooperation. By major institutions I understand the political constitution and the principal economic and social arrangements."[6]

Justice, then, is the basic principle and is dominant over other principles in Rawls's form of ethics. Rawls begins his theory with a definition of the individual or citizen and states:

> Each person possesses an inviolability founded on justice that even the welfare of society as a whole cannot override. For this reason justice denies that the loss of freedom for

some is made right by the greater good shared by others. It does not allow that the sacrifices imposed on a few are outweighed by the larger sum of advantages enjoyed by many. Therefore, in a just society the liberties of equal citizenship are taken as settled; the rights secured by justice are not subject to political bargaining or to the calculus of social interest.[7]

In developing his theory, Rawls suggests an intellectual device or technique by which the principles of equity can be set forth. The first and most important intellectual technique is the notion of original position. The original position constitutes an agreement upon the most basic principles of justice upon which all of the basic structures of society (social, economic, and political) will be predicated. The principles of justice that emerge are both final and binding on all: "Since the original agreement is final and made in perpetuity, there is no second chance."[8] In this intellectual condition, it is necessary to have what Rawls calls a veil of ignorance, described as follows:

> First of all, no one knows his place in society, his class, position or social status; nor does he know his fortune in the distribution of natural assets or abilities, his intelligence and strengths, and the like. Nor, again, does anyone know his conception of the good, the particulars of his rational plan of life, or even the special features of his psychology such as his aversion to risk or liability to optimism or pessimism. More than this, I assume that the parties do not know the particular circumstances of their own society. That is, they do not know its economic or political situation, or the level of civilization and culture it has been able to achieve. The persons in the original position have no information as to which generation they belong.[9]

Obviously, anyone working out rules for social, economic, and political behavior under the concept of original position and with the veil of ignorance would take care to formulate rules that would be acceptable to themselves regardless of their station in society at any time. David K. Hart interprets Rawls this way: "Not knowing specific conditions, they do not know whether they will be among the more advantaged, or the less advantaged. Wisdom dictates, then, that the principles of justice chosen must advance the condition of the least advantaged man, since one could easily be that man."[10]

To make this theory operative, Rawls then proposes two principles of justice: "The first principle is to have an equal right to the most extensive total system of equal basic liberties compatible with a similar system of liberty for all. The second principle is that social and economic inequalities are to be arranged so that they are both: (a) to the greatest benefit to the least advantaged, consistent with the just savings principle, and (b) attached to offices and positions open to all under conditions of fair equality and opportunity."[11]

These two principles, then, are to be a right of the same significance or order as the present rights as we understand them in government. Hart further states:

> According to Rawls, acceptance of the two principles of justice means that the collective efforts of society would be concentrated in behalf of its less advantaged members. This does not mean that all inequalities would disappear and all good will be equally distributed to achieve parity throughout the society. There would still be disparities in income and status. But there is an irreducible minimum of *primary goods* (such as self-respect, rights and liberties, power and opportunities, income and wealth) that are due every man, and the minimum must be met.[12]

Rawls states that this is "a strongly egalitarian conception in the sense that unless there is a distribution that makes both persons better off (limiting ourselves to the two-person case for simplicity), an equal distribution is to be preferred."[13]

David Hart argues that self-respect is the most important of the primary goals to which Rawls referred. He states that "nothing must be allowed to lessen the self-respect in any man, nor may any man be treated instrumentally . . . thus, every social institution or action must enhance the self-respect of every person, whether the least advantaged or most advantaged, since individual self-respect is the foundation of a just society."[14]

It is obvious that Rawls's theory of justice is vastly different from other contemporary patterns of moral reasoning. Rawls does not argue it because it is good or right but rather because there is an increasing importance to the interdependence of persons that makes notions of advantages and disadvantages less and less acceptable. It is a pervasive sense of noblesse oblige or a sense of eternity among people. Rawls states that "in justice as fairness men agree to share one another's fate. In designing institutions they undertake to avail themselves of the accidents of nature and social circumstances only when doing so is for the common benefit."[15] Because not all persons are genetically "equal," the more advantaged have a moral duty to serve all others including the disadvantaged, not for altruistic reasons but because of the significance of human interdependence. As Hart says, "One serves because justice requires it and the result is the continuous enhancement of self-respect. Just actions, then, not only create the optimal condition for human life, they also are a major element in the rationalization of self."[16]

Although all of this theory and definition is interesting, we live in a world of large and very complex organizations where the application of such concepts is difficult. This is also a world in which organizations tend to elevate their own needs over individual needs and goals. The problem is one of making complex organizations responsible to the needs of the individual. This requires rising above the rules and routines of organization to some concern for the self-respect and dignity of the individual citizen. Rawls's theory is designed to instruct those who administer organizations that the rights of individuals would be everywhere protected.

Hart summarizes this approach to social equity with the following: (1) The theory of justice would provide social equity with an ethical content. Acceptance of the theory of justice would provide the equitable public administrator with clear, well-developed ethical guidelines which would give social equity the force that it now lacks. (2) The theory of justice could provide the necessary ethical consensus—that the equitable public administrator has both the duty and the obligation to deploy his efforts on behalf of the less advantaged. (3) The theory of justice would impose constraints upon all complex public organizations since no organization would be allowed to infringe upon the basic liberties of individuals. (4) The theory of justice would provide a means to resolve ethical impasses (the original position). (5) The theory of justice would provide a professional code for public administration that would require a commitment to social equity.[17]

Internal Equity

All of this might be nice theoretically, but what does it mean in practice? In fact, our government systems are increasingly moving toward the principles of social equity being set forth here. But the irony is that the real impetus toward social equity in public service has come not from public administration or from the executive branch or the legislative branches, but from the courts. To be sure, the national government in 1940 passed the Ramspeck Act, which prohibited discrimination in federal employment based on race, creed, or color, and most states have followed. It has taken the courts, however, to establish social equity as a fact.

One of the landmark cases is *Griggs* v. *Duke Power*.[18] In this case, laborers were required to be high school graduates and to pass aptitude tests to engage in low skill occupations in more desirable divisions of the company's functioning. The clear effect of the selection policy was to concentrate blacks in a lower paid "labor division" of the Duke Power Company because, by percentage, far fewer blacks are high school graduates and able to pass the two aptitude tests. The company could not prove that high school graduation or the passage of aptitude tests were accurate predictors of job performance. As a consequence, unlawful discimination was found to exist and ordered to be corrected. Note Chief Justice Warren Burger's opinion summarizing the court's position, particularly with respect to how it compares with Rawls's theory of justice:

> Nothing in the Act (1964 Civil Rights Act) precludes the use of testing or measuring procedures; obviously, they are useful. What Congress has forbidden is giving these devices and mechanisms controlling force unless they are demonstrably a reasonable measure of job performance. Congress has not commanded that the less qualified be preferred over the better qualified simply because of minority origins. Far from disparaging job qualifications as such, Congress has made such qualifications a controlling factor, so that race, religion, nationality and sex become irrelevant. What Congress has commanded is that *any* tests used must measure the person for the job and not the person in the abstract.[19]

Following *Griggs*, there has been a spate of similar cases. Eugene McGregor has summarized these cases: "Where selection practices are shown to have a differential effect for minorities, the courts do not hesitate to enjoin or change those practices which do not clear rational or empirical validity. Second, aptitude tests and educational degrees appear to be the most vulnerable selection devices for policemen, firemen and other occupational sectors where administrative and scientific skill is not an initial job requirement."[20]

The courts are less vigorous and less definitive when it comes to jobs that are administrative, professional, and technical in nature. In such jobs, it is difficult to define precisely what the person does and, therefore, difficult to be precise about what constitutes appropriate preparation. Thus, the current battles for social equity frequently involve upper-level positions.

If it is assumed that social equity is desirable, is there a practical way of directing and distributing things equitably? Again, the courts and not public administration practice or theory answered this question. Regarding the question of equity in the general distribution of public service, the landmark case is *Hawkins* v. *Town of Shaw*.[21] In Shaw, Mississippi, municipal services are financed from general tax revenues. Mr. Hawkins, a black man, was able to demonstrate that the distribution of sidewalks, paved streets, street lighting, sewerage services, and the like was significantly greater in the white than the black sections of the town of Shaw. The court found no constitutional justification for residents who were similarly taxed to have fewer street lights, paved streets, and sewers and less police protection. The town of Shaw was ordered to develop and present to the court an equitable plan for the distribution of public services to all of its citizens.

The two critical cases in the distribution of educational services based on property taxes reached different conclusions. In *Serrano* v. *Priest*, a California case, the state was ordered to reorganize the financing of public education to ensure that wealthy and poor school districts balanced their expenditures so that poorer children did not by definition receive poorer educations.[22] In a Texas case, *Rodriguez* v. *San Antonio*, the U.S. Supreme Court concluded that the system of local property taxation to support schools is unfair and inequitable, but not unconstitutional.[23] The question then is: if it is unfair and inequitable, what responsibility do school superintendents, school boards, state commissioners of education, and other public officials in education have to correct the situation by applying principles of social equity?

Stephen R. Chitwood has given detailed consideration to this subject.[24] An infinite number of patterns might be used to distribute public services. They might be reduced to three basic forms: first, equal services to all; second, proportionally equal services to all; and third, unequal services to individuals corresponding to relevant differences.

Equal services to all has, in Chitwood's judgment, limited applicability. In the first place, most government services cannot be equally utilized by all citizens because services are initially designed to serve the needs of a restricted clientele—compulsory education for younger people, for example. And, of course, there would be insufficient funds to provide all services to all people.

Proportional equality suggests a formula for distribution of services based on some specified characteristic presumably connected to need. For example, the number of uniformed policemen assigned to patrol particular areas may vary according to crime rate. Public assistance may vary according to number of dependents. Chitwood argues that "providing public services on a proportionally equal basis seems both pragmatically and humanistically appealing. On pragmatic ground it provides apparently concrete, objective bases for allocating services among the populace; and on the humanistic side, it allows more services to be provided as their perceived need increases."

In the case of unequal public services, according to Chitwood, individuals receive services in amounts corresponding to relevant differences in some characteristic possessed by those recipients. There are several such criteria. One might be the ability to pay. Using ability to pay, one would argue that city libraries, parks, and other public facilities be put in the more affluent sections of the city because those citizens pay more taxes. A second criteria would be the providing of services on the basis of need, and in this case, parks, libraries, and other public facilities would be located in the less affluent parts of town on the justification that the need is greater there and the citizens living in those regions would be less able to pay to have library, park, or other services. Using this example, it is likely that an equitable public administrator would incline in the direction of need in the distribution of services, at least according to the definitions of social equity set out in the first part of this chapter. It could be further argued that basic or minimum living standards constitute an almost obligatory service to include nutrition, shelter, clothing, health care, employment, education, and other minimally acceptable levels of existence.

Chitwood also sets out the difference between vertical and horizontal equity. Both vertical and horizontal equity are applicable to the three dimensions of equity described just above. Vertical equity has to do with criteria for distributing services among heterogeneous people. Under vertical equity, an effort would be made to devise a rationale or criterion for allocating services among differing groups of citizens, say, by sex, age, geographic location, income, and the like. The absence or presence of a given personal attribute, say, wealth, would determine in part the level of services received. Under conditions of horizontal equity, the principle would be to provide equal treatment for equals, say, for example, the annual dollar expenditures for the education of students in the first grade across an entire state would be approximately equal.

Obviously, questions of social equity will be central to future policy decisions in public administration. It is incumbent on the public servant to be able to develop and defend criteria and measures of equity and to understand the impact of public services on the dignity and well-being of citizens. It would follow that concepts of social equity would come to be fundamental in the education of modern public administrators. So, too, will concerns for the responsiveness of complex organizations to the needs of both the individuals working in them and the citizens who are receiving their services. This will oblige the public administrator to be deeply concerned for the social consequences of his or her work. The public servant will very likely be an advocate, but most modern public servants already are. Frequently, however, their advocacy has to do with given public services such as fire, police, national defense, environment, and the like. From now on, it will be essential to relate the public servant's substantive field to questions of equity and social well-being. This should cause the administrator to be far more participatory and open in the management of government agencies. It is difficult to know of citizen needs if the administrator is not in direct and routine interaction with elected officials and legislative bodies. Thus, participation and political interaction are critical to the development of the concept of social equity. The public official will come to be understood as a processor and facilitator with elected officials of government response to rapid social, economic, and political change. In fact, an ability to mobilize government institutions to change may well come to define leadership in the future. The public servant will not be a hero or a Don Quixote, but rather a master of mobilizing and distributing public services fairly and equitably when such services are needed and discontinuing them when they are not needed. This does not promise more than can be given nor does it imply unbridled government intervention. Indeed, just the reverse. The public servant, with elected officials and legislative bodies, will plan the processes of change in a systematic way, keeping front and center a dialogue over what it is that government properly ought to be doing and for whom it ought to be done. Only with such a dialogue can the administrator hope to function rationally.

In their recent assessment of education for public service, Richard Chapman and Frederic N. Cleaveland call for the development of a new "public service ethic."[25] Chapman and Cleaveland do not attempt to define that ethic and suggest, wisely, that such an ethic must evolve and must always be a product of the blending of the values associated with public service. The traditional values of public administration—economy, efficiency, effectiveness, responsiveness to elected officials, responsibility—have served us well. But the experiences of the past decade indicate that other values (not necessarily new ones) are important to any public service ethic. Certainly citizen responsiveness, worker and citizen participation in the decision process, the equitable distribution of public services, the provision of a range of citizen choices, and administrative responsibility for program effectiveness are values that suit our times. If there is, or even if there ought to be, a public service ethic, these values are as compelling as are the better understood commitments to managerial values.

This is not a negation of the importance of a general public service productivity or of the continuing search for efficiencies and economies in government. It is simply to suggest that the most productive governments, the most efficient governments, and the most economizing governments can still be perpetuating poverty, inequality of opportunity, and injustice. Both the classic bureaucratic model and the neobureaucratic model offer little in the way of offsetting those tendencies. Therefore, modern public administration will search both theoretically and normatively for what Vincent Ostrom calls "democratic administration."[26]

4: Statics and
Dynamics in
Public Administration

Harmony, simplicity, provision for change,
decentralization, and responsibility,
represented not only characteristics of
good administration as understood by Jefferson,
but they describe standards to which good
government ought always attempt to conform.
—Lynton K. Caldwell, "Thomas Jefferson
and Public Administration"

New public administration has been introduced with some detail and definition and has been placed in context. But what is to be the future of public administration? If new public administration is change oriented, what types of changes are being suggested and sought and why? How do these proposed changes relate to the traditions of the field and to our concepts and theories? And what does all of this mean for the way we manage in the public service and for the approaches we use for designing government organizations? What are likely to be the social consequences of these changes? What will be the effects of these changes on education for public service? These questions are the subjects of Chapters 4, 5, and 6. In this chapter we deal with the statics and dynamics of public administration. Three subjects will be treated here—change and responsiveness; administrative rationality and management; worker/management-citizen relations. These subjects are set out in terms of classic or traditional thinking, represented by the "from" column in the tables that follow and by contemporary thinking represented by the "transition" column in these tables; future projections are represented by the "to" column.

Change and Responsiveness

Public organizations have always faced a basic dilemma. They are customarily organized to accomplish a given task or to deliver a particular service, and they are expected to be stable, ordered, predictable, anchored to a permanent funding source, and occupying a particular niche in the public sector. The organization has a staff, records, procedures, and policies, all of which result in order and stability. But the public organization is situated in a dynamic and rapidly changing environment—an environment to which it must respond. Both in the theory and the practice of public administration, we have dealt with this dilemma in two ways: first, by reorganization, and second, by human relations techniques. Simply put, we can try to change the organization (reorganization) or we can try to change the people in the organization (human relations). Both of these approaches are important and have demonstrated an ability to bring about organizational change. The problem is that neither the theory nor the practice of public administration has very effectively codified the manner in which this process occurs, at least in terms of the public organization being a rational organism. Most of the basic studies of organizational behavior focus on stability and patterns of predictable behavior. These studies found a process of goal displacement, as in the case of the police department with a goal of law enforcement replacing that goal with goals having to do with organizational survival or well-being. Victor Thompson, James Thompson, and Anthony Downs were looking for stability and goal displacement, and they found it.[1] They did not study change or responsiveness.

The best study of reorganization is Frederick C. Mosher's *Governmental Reorganizations: Cases and Commentary*, in which it was demonstrated that under certain circumstances, organizations can become more rational or goal-oriented either by changing their structures or rearranging their staff.[2] Similarly, studies of human relations training programs indicate that organizational rationality can be enhanced by such techniques.

Events of the decade of the 1970s seem to have shifted both the theory and practice of public administration to the application of some cosmetics to change processes. For example, it is now common to think in terms of reorganization as a fairly routine activity, and the discussion of organizational change, and/or "planned organization change" is commonplace. We appear, then, no longer to be of the view that once the organization is corrected it is therefore correct, at least for the near-term future. Similarly, the present view seems to be that organizations should attempt to respond to rapid social change. Hence we see programs such as affirmative action, or fair employment practices, or major kinds of reorganizations occurring. Some of the more dramatic of these have to do with the so-called third sector by which public organizations presume to "correct" things either by "privatization" as in the case of COMSAT or the "Postal Service" or "publicization," as in the case of AMTRACK (to use only federal government examples). This has been done by the relatively traditional "problem-solving" approach. It is also "responsive" in the sense that it is an attempt to deal with some or another kind of social, political, or economic problem.

Public administration appears to be in a transitory state, between a classic need to be organized, predictable, productive, and stable on the one hand, and to be responsive, adaptive, and changeable on the other.

Public administration, however, has not been able to articulate a concept of change and responsiveness that fully describes means by which organizations are being or can be made responsive. In addition to an inability to articulate a concept of responsiveness, public organizations have been generally unable to counter the findings of the research that seems to indicate that some social problems are endemic and seem to resist "being solved," irrespective of the quality or quantity of public service designed to solve them. The Jencks research on primary and secondary education shows that the quality of schooling (dollars spent per child, quality of teachers, and so on) "has less of an effect on educational outcomes or the productivity of the educational system than do such factors such as social status or family stability."[3] Similar arguments are made for virtually every public service, but particularly those public services for which it is especially difficult to measure productivity or effectiveness. It is possible therefore to argue that spending half as much for police would have no discernible effect on either the level of the commission of crimes or the capacity to apprehend those who commit crimes. Still, when pressed, it is unlikely that anyone is prepared to sustain the argument that there is absolutely no need for law enforcement, not to mention education, social service, national defense, and many other parts of the public sector for which it is difficult to demonstrate productivity.

It is a "best guess," therefore, that over the next few years public administration will give significant and practical and intellectual energy to the subject of change and responsiveness. Based on observing successful planned organizational change, it is likely that public administration will come to a common understanding that reorganization is not the same as change. Further, it may become the accepted view that reorganizing at a time of crisis is not what ought to be done. What is likely to develop is a set of criteria for a given segment of the public sector (say, law enforcement) by which the effectiveness of a particular organization is judged. Along with these criteria will likely emerge an institutionalized means of bringing about change. These means could be as simple as the contractual arrangements one sees in local government or with the Defense Department or NASA, or may resemble much of what is now going on under the label "productivity bargaining." The point is that economic, political, and social change is now so rapid that the only way organizations can be responsive is to develop criteria by which they can judge effectiveness and then to institutionalize procedures by which changes, and often fairly rapid changes, can be made so as to make the organization capable of being responsive. This will require the organization to articulate its criteria and develop its institutionalized change procedures, and these procedures will have to be stable, predictable, and anchored. It will not necessarily be the form or structure or staff of the organization that is its basic manifestation of stability, but the agreed-upon criteria for effectiveness and procedures for change.

If this prediction is accurate, it must be assumed that not all organizations will "grow" or "develop." Indeed, it is now commonly understood both in the practice and the teaching of public administration that there is a fundamental difference between growth and change as phenomena. Growth and its reverse, decline, is a transitory phenomenon, whereas change is the eternal dynamic. Consequently, it would be a best guess that we are as likely to engage in the management of declining organizations as we are in the management of growing organizations. The point is that in either case, the organizations are able more effectively to handle the phenomenon of change. Therefore, whereas in the 1960s it was commonplace to speak of increments and development, in the 1970s we speak as much of decrements and devolution. The problem is that our theories as well as our heritage cause us to be inclined to increments and development, rather than decrements and devolution. We know better how to manage growth as a form of change than decline as a form of change. It is a best guess that over the near-term future we will be forced to learn to be more effective managers of decrements and devolution.

The future context of public administration will dictate the emphasis on decline and devolution as forms of change. Our entire government system will be changing, but it will not likely be growing, at least not growing as it has in the past. We will increasingly be a service or postindustrial economy—and the government will either provide or regulate services. We will be at or near zero population growth. Our population will be getting older, indicating a shift from education to health care as issues and probably a shift in expenditures. We will continue to have acute problems of economic distribution and employment in the United States.

And we will have problems of distribution between the United States and other nations. Our energy sources will decline. We will be changing, and changing very rapidly. But in many sectors of the public service we will not be growing and probably will be declining. Can the theory and practice of public administration accommodate our new context?

There is a close relationship between organizational change and what is ordinarily referred to as "science and technology" in public administration. It is increasingly apparent that although we are technologically advanced, we are also politically and administratively advanced. Our problem is that we tend to approach the need for change as if it were mostly a technological or scientific activity. The reverse is in fact true. Change as the eternal dynamic in public administration is mostly a political and managerial phenomenon. To be sure, change has technological and scientific aspects, but it is increasingly apparent that technology is not synonymous with change. There could be no better example than water and air pollution. This is a technologically "caused" problem, we continue to search for technological solutions, and in this field our technology is certainly improving. But pollution of air and water is most effectively dealt with politically and administratively first, as the means by which we decide to apply a given technology. The environmental impact statement is an administrative and political tool. As a best guess, public administration will continue to question the correlation between technology and change and will come increasingly to understand how to use administrative and political approaches to change.

In any discussion of change and responsiveness, one must address the question of "responsiveness to whom?" In the traditions of public administration, the notion of responsiveness had particularly to do with sensing a need or a force and mounting an effective adaption. The problem is that the public service functions in the context of an electoral democracy and a representative form of government, coupled with pluralistic centers of power. To be responsive to "the majority" and also be responsive to the needs of an underprivileged minority and at the same time be responsive to powerful minorities is asking the impossible. Consequently, public organizations steer a careful course between (1) a general adaption to changes in elected representatives and executives, which constitutes a low-level form of responsiveness to the majority will; and (2) working with minority or interest groups, which usually results in a pattern of relatively effective response to particularized needs. The problem has been the lack of a pattern of responsiveness to nonpowerful or disorganized minorities. This has been dealt with in most recent years by widespread patterns of participation, some feigned or rigged, and much of it basically for purposes of cooptation. A best guess is that future forms of responsiveness will more fully involve citizens and constituents so they can both effect policy and cause adaption on the part of the public agency. Short-term tactics such as the ombudsman, little city halls, citizen review committees, and the like are just that—short-term. It is likely that we shall continue to see movements in the direction of a kind of semi-integration of citizens and constituents with so-called "street-level bureaucracies" that should elicit relatively rapid adaption to the needs of given groups of citizens. Much of the movement toward decentralization and toward "neighborhood control" is beginning to have an effect on service-type organizations. It is doubtful if the same effect will be felt by organizations that are not in a service posture. It is more difficult, for example, for the Department of Health and Human Services or the Department of Housing and Urban Development to be responsive to the needs of a neighborhood than it is, say, for a school district, a police department, or a neighborhood health center. Table 3 is a simplified summary of these points.[4]

The Civil Service Reform Act of 1978 is the most important change in federal public administration in decades. This reform exhibits a new public administration perspective in the field of personnel administration. In the ninety plus years of the civil service system in the national government, the personnel system had moved far beyond the need to stamp out the spoils system. The civil service has become

Table 3. Change and Responsiveness in New Public Administration

From	Transition	To
The problem is basically one of reform or change (putting right that which is wrong).*	Change and reorganization should be encouraged.	The problem is one of institutionalizing change procedures (recognizing that those things put right are unlikely to stay right and making correctability criteria as important as correctness).
Rapid social change is a transient phenomenon needing to be weathered and adjusted to.*	Organization must attempt to respond to rapid social change (reduce lag).	Rapid social change is a permanent phenomenon needing to be facilitated and capitalized upon.
The problems occasioned by uncertainty, complexity, and rapidity of change require larger investments in organizational machinery increments and development.*	The problems occasioned by uncertainty, complexity, and rapidity of change require modifying already established machinery.	The problems occasioned by uncertainty, complexity, and rapidity of change require larger investments in decrements and devolution.
"Responsiveness" requires effective scanning of open information within the organization so it can sense when adaption is required.*	"Responsiveness" requires widespread participation by clients, chiefly for purposes of cooptation.	"Responsiveness" requires effective scanning of clients and constituents so that they can elicit adaption when it is required.
Leadership by authority.	Leadership by consent.	Leadership by change facilitation.

(continued)

*Indicates a statement from Robert J. Biller, "Converting Knowledge into Action: Toward a Postindustrial Society," in Jong S. Jun and William B. Storm, eds., *Tomorrow's Organizations: Challenges and Strategies* (Glenville, Ill.: Scott, Foresman, 1973).

Table 3, continued

From	Transition	To
Technology may provide the solution to politically "caused" problems.*	Politics must accommodate technological solutions.	Politics may provide the solution to technologically "caused" problems.

*Indicates a statement from Robert J. Biller, "Converting Knowledge into Action: Toward a Postindustrial Society," in Jong S. Jun and William B. Storm, eds., *Tomorrow's Organizations: Challenges and Strategies* (Glenville, Ill.: Scott, Foresman, 1973).

very large, ponderously slow, and preoccupied with the protection of the government employee as against the policy and management needs of the government. All of the techniques of personnel administration—testing, position descriptions, eligibility lists, pay schedules, equal pay for equal work, veterans preferences, grievances, and most recently unionization—have risen to a level of utilization so great as to significantly impair the ability of the national government to be responsive, to change, to be productive, or to be effectively managed. The purposes of government have come to be less important than the techniques of personnel administration.

The Civil Service Reform Act of 1978 separates the monolithic U.S. Civil Service Commission into three agencies, the Office of Personnel Management, the Merit System Protection Board, and the Federal Labor Relations Authority. The Office of Personnel Management is responsible for the testing, position description, and other personnel functions of the government including the maintenance of a new Senior Executive Service. The Merit System Protection Board is to handle the grievances of civil servants on matters such as promotions, pay, work assignments, and the like. The Federal Labor Relations Authority handles the collective bargaining process of federal agencies.

Under this reform, the civil service is being significantly decentralized. Managers now work with their employees to set the standards of performance or productivity. Rewards for excellent work are available as are easier systems of both reprimand and dismissal for ineffectiveness. Changes in position and tasks are much easier to make—making the government potentially more responsive. The individual manager has much more influence over the employee and, therefore, can now be fairly held responsible for the effectiveness of his or her unit.

The new Senior Executive Service is composed of 98.5 percent of federal employees in the general schedule ranks of 16 through 18, the top 8,000 officials in the federal government. They now have much less job security than they once did. Thus, if they do not perform effectively, they may be dismissed. And these top officials are now eligible for merit pay that can range as high as 50 percent of salary based upon performance. The Senior Executive can even qualify for the title Meritorious Executive with a $10,000 bonus or Distinguished Executive with a $20,000 bonus. These top officials are no longer permanently assigned to a particular agency (rank in the job) but may now be moved to the agency where they are most particularly needed or may be most effective (rank in the person). No more than 10 percent of the Senior Executive Service may be made up of political appointees, so 90 percent of them are career government professionals. This reform promises to develop a much more responsive, changeable, and effective group of top-level executives.

This civil service reform is interesting in several respects. First, it is a mix of reorganization, the restructuring of agencies, bureaus, offices, and reform, the implementation of new or difference concepts and principles. Both are necessary to effective change and particularly to the continuing ability of the government to be both organized and changeful. Second, the reform has been almost totally political and administrative. The technologies of traditional civil service have given way to concepts and principles of modern administration and the need for policy responsiveness. Third, and perhaps most interesting, this reform was guided by Alan K. (Scotty) Campbell who developed this reform with other scholars and practitioners of public administration. And, he and his colleagues guided the processes of political and administrative adoption of these reforms. Campbell is possibly the archetypical public administrator who leads by facilitating the processes of change.

Rationality

If there is a subject basic to the practice and theory of public administration it is rationality. The conscious application of knowledge to achieve a generally agreed-upon objective is fundamental to the field. There are sundry interpretations of rationality, to include the old policy-administration dichotomy, followed closely by the policy-administration continuum. This was followed by the so-called positivist model that posits a management science and a kind of pure rationality, most generally associated with Herbert Simon.[5] The reverse of the positivist view is the so-called incrementalist (now we can also say decrementalist) view, fully set out by Charles Lindbloom.[6] Amitai Etzioni suggested a third approach which he calls mixed scanning, a compromise position.[7] The middle position, Etzioni argues, is necessary because the rational view provides too much power to the decision makers, whereas the incremental view provides too little. The mixed scanning approach sets up a two-level process by which fundamental decisions can be dealt with by a lens that sees in depth and deals with the problem fundamentally and by a wide-angle approach that deals with the problems at the margins, or incrementally. Quite clearly, the incremental or decremental view is the most empirically accurate of the approaches to rationality. It may not, however, be the most productive in terms of achieving effective, efficient, or equitable administration.

The experiences of the past ten years should serve as thundering evidence that we can make mistakes in the application of knowledge and that professional or administrative rationality is not necessarily what the citizens wish. It seems possible for every subset of the public sector (the police, the social services, national defense) successfully to sustain the view that what they do is desirable. It is also obvious, however, that government and the public organizations that make the government work can do only so much. Consequently, choices must be made as to what the government is to do. Each public service profession (or occupation) would presume to know what is the best for the public. In their rationality, their goals are desirable, and they know how to achieve them, so it is simply a matter of spending the money to get on with the job.

Not so.

It appears likely that we are moving toward a different concept of rationality in public administration. This concept is not an easy one to articulate, in part because it is not yet formed in practice (theory often follows practice in an applied field such as public administration). Tomorrow's rationality is likely, however, to work from a set of new premises: (1) We know how to do things. (2) Many of those things we are now doing. (3) There is an already established infrastructure (the complexity of public service organizations) to do these things. (4) The public servants doing these things and in these organizations are committed to these things. (5) But we do not have a national or even a local agreement as to what needs to be done. (6) To some extent, the electoral system is a process of determining what ought to be done. (7) And, to some extent, all previous commitments constitute a determination of what ought to be done. We should educate, we should defend ourselves, we should keep the law. (8) But, beyond these rather vague goals, there is widespread disagreement as to how to achieve them. (9) So, public administration should be the means by which professionals, elected officials, and citizens decide which activities are most valued and relate most generally to agreed-upon goals.

From these premises can come a very simple kind of rationality. For purposes of labeling, let's call it "buffered rationality." Buffered is used here to describe the best effects of rationality, but stripped of some of its undesirable side effects. In buffered rationality there may be general agreement as to the need for schools. This does not mean that there is agreement as to what constitutes education or what exactly those schools ought to be doing. We presumably know how to educate although we now know there are serious limitations on what we always presumed to be our capabilities in this field. The same could be said for law enforcement and national defense, based on experiences in the recent past. Therefore, buffered rationality would argue that a shorter-term, less fundamental approach contains fewer social and political risks and is probably better suited to public organizations. It might be rational for police officials and citizens to work out a particular patrolling procedure, which they might collectively regard as acceptable. This approach avoids either the assumption that the citizens know everything about how patrolling ought to be done, or that the police know it all. Buffered rationality, then, would seek to develop commitment to what is, in the short term, a sensible and agreeable activity, assuming that this activity falls within the general range of loosely agreed-upon overall objectives. To follow the above example, it is assumed that high-quality law enforcement is a generally agreed-upon objective. Let's further assume that the maintenance of a police department is similarly agreeable. In this rationality there would be a need to develop a commitment and consensus to the activities of the police department so as to make the police as an institution, and law enforcement as an overall objective, generally acceptable.

So, to some extent, the concept of rationality has been turned on its head. No doubt some theorists will be appalled at this argument, but it seems the only way to articulate what happens when effective public administration occurs. This position is being taken for a variety of reasons. First, we have learned how remarkably complex public systems are. Second, we have also learned by sad experience the danger of the application of knowledge and technology for which there is not a consensus. If nothing else, the wars in Korea and in Vietnam should have made that clear. Third, it is now more obvious to us that experimentation ought to be done as just that—social experimentation. For some reason public officials who know how to do things also assume to know what should be done. They, along with elected officials, have a tendency to seek to apply more than they really know. If applied in an organizational context, and if what is applied is nonsense, the social, economic, and political backlash can be severe.

In buffered rationality, planning is closely wedded to action. The isolation of planners from doers probably was wrongheaded anyway. The same could be said for policy analysis. The extremes of the planner or the policy analyst are usually badly muted or buffered by experience. So in buffered rationality, our best guess is that we will first seek to develop commitment to sensible activities and thereby receive some assurances of at least a modicum of overall objectives. Second, we will embrace planning and policy analysis as a part of the processes of developing commitment to sensible action and not as a side activity based on traditional rationality by which it was decided in some analytical fashion what was to be done. Third, we probably will be less willing to say we know what the results will be when in fact we do not. Fourth, we will continue to be able to do things effectively, because that's the basic purpose of public administration. Fifth, we will give more attention to trying to discover or determine what ought to be done and by whom.

Some would argue that this approach to rationality has in fact neutralized public administration. Not so. But what it does say is that there are limits to the practice of public administration, and to its effectiveness, and that we are increasingly aware of our metes and bounds. This should not make public administration any less of a challenge. In fact, it makes it all the more interesting. Harlan Cleveland puts it very well when he argues that "if planning is improvisation in a general sense of direction, then the executive leader's primary task is to establish, maintain, advertise, and continuously amend a sense of direction that his colleagues in complexity can share. The conviction that the goals that he helps set are possible of achievement is an indispensable part of his psyche. His is the optimism of the doer and, warranted by the experience of others, justified by his own determination to organize a future with a difference."[8] This approach is described in Table 4.

Table 4. Rationality in New Public Administration

From	Transition	To
Public administration is deciding what you want to do and building an increasingly institutionalized organization to do it.*	Build the institution, then change it and the people in it.	You start by doing something and codify an organization's way of doing it and the value attached to it only to the extent warranted by the stability (tranquillity/turbulence) of the problem faced.
We know what ought to be done; the problem is discovering how to do it well.*		We know how to do things; the problem is discovering how to determine what ought to be done.
We know more than we apply; the problem is one of transmitting this knowledge more efficiently to consumers.*	We are uncertain in our knowledge, so we experiment with consumers. The experiment becomes the institution.	We know less than we apply; the problem is one of trying to prevent the transmitting of nonsense to consumers.
Planning is a crisis technique.	Planning is an institutionalized process.	Planning is acting.
Set sensible goals, then institutionalize to achieve them.*	Seek to develop commitment to sensible goals in order to achieve sensible and consistent action.	Seek to develop commitment to sensible action in order to achieve sensible overall objectives.

*Indicates a statement from Robert J. Biller, "Converting Knowledge into Action: Toward a Postindustrial Society," in Jong S. Jun and William B. Storm, eds., *Tomorrow's Organizations: Challenges and Strategies* (Glenville, Ill.: Scott, Foresman, 1973).

New approaches to rationality and to the processes of administrative change are illustrated by the work of the President's Management Improvement Council in the Jimmy Carter administration. When compared with traditional approaches, the differences are stark. For example, the Louis Brownlow Committee (the President's Committee on Administrative Management) in the Roosevelt administration (1937) focused on the Executive Office of the President and dealt with issues such as the number of persons and functions reporting directly to the president (span of control) and improved methods of budgeting and other executive controls. While the president's cabinet serves as one form of coordinating mechanism, the Brownlow Committee recommended the strengthening of the President's immediate staff for purposes of planning, direction, communication; these activities were to be carried out by many key assistants with "a passion for anonymity." The Brownlow Committee also recommended the full extension of "merit principles" to virtually the entire civil service. Most of the recommendations of the Brownlow Committee were adopted and have since been developed as important aspects of the national government.

The Brownlow Committee was followed by the first Hoover (Herbert) Commission (Commission on Organization of the Executive Branch of the Government) in the Harry S. Truman administration (1949). The findings and recommendations tended to confirm the work of its predecessor. In sum they recommended that a strengthened presidency (almost a corporate analog) will result in improvements all down the line. The second Hoover Commission in the Eisenhower administration (1955) dealt primarily with the proper structuring of the functions of government (should the Forest Service remain in the U.S. Department of Agriculture or be placed in the U.S. Department of Interior, and perhaps integrated with the Bureau of Land Management in Interior?). In the 1950s and 1960s many state and local governments developed "little Hoover Commissions" that engaged in similar reviews of the structures and functions of government at their level.

The work of the Brownlow Committee and the two Hoover Commissions was based on traditional administrative principles: a limited span of control, a clean and uncluttered chain of command, a strong executive able to use the full range of management controls; a logical grouping of areas, agencies, and departments where common policy fields (such as forests and land) could be organizationally linked. And they worked from traditional definitions of rationality as described earlier in this chapter.

By contrast, the current President's Management Improvement Council (PMIC) is significantly less concerned with what goes on in the Executive Offices, if proper public administration principles are being followed or if the units of the national government are properly aligned with each other. What the PMIC is interested in is working with agency heads, the Comptroller General (the General Accounting Office—not, strictly speaking, an executive agency but an agency of the U.S. Congress), senior program managers, and administrative officials generally to study activities of the government, recommend improvements, and implement those improvements. Specific projects are carried out using agency representatives, members of the Council, talent from other agencies and from industry, state and local government, universities, and public interest groups. The procedures may be rather analytical (costs versus benefits, productivity, effectiveness) but involve a commitment to completing a "management improvement" or a change, rather than merely studying a problem. The projects undertaken are selected, to some extent, on the basis of their potential for change. It is not assumed that the basic solution to problems is more staff, a larger agency, more agency autonomy, or a bigger budget—these being the standard solutions to management and policy problems. The intent is that the Council, in the longer term, will become a forum for the exchange of ideas and information about what may be effective in improving government effectiveness. One of the objectives is the development of policies and approaches that will result in stronger and more permanent management improvement systems.

The cochairmen of the Council are James T. McIntyre, Jr., director of the Office of Management and Budget, and Alan K. Campbell, director of the Office of Personnel Management; the director of the Council is Charles Bingman. All three are experienced professional managers and policy experts. The approach they have chosen closely parallels the logic of the new public administration. Change procedures are being institutionalized and the general criteria for change being developed. The processes of change are being geared up to respond to the rapidity of social economics and technological change. Change is being identified as an important leadership responsibility. The change process is one of deciding the value of government activities and the extent to which generally agreed upon governmental goals are being met. The people studying governmental activities and planning changes are, to an appreciable extent, those who will carry out the changes. Planning, then, is a part of management, as is the process of change.

Management-Worker, Management-Citizen Relations

The reader may think it strange to put together the subjects of relations between supervisors and subordinates and relations between public agencies and citizens. It would be difficult to sustain the argument that these are the same things, because they are not. They are put together not because they are logical or theoretical cousins, but because they are cousins in style and approach.

Perhaps the most empirically rich subject in organization theory is concerned with those aspects of administrative behavior having to do with applications of authority, questions of job satisfaction, and relations between managers and workers. Most of the evidence of this research indicates that morale as well as productivity are enhanced by non-authoritarian approaches to management, by consciously developed approaches to worker involvement in the decision process, and by the development of democratic work environments. Both practitioners and theorists might find themselves generally agreeing that this is the direction public administration is moving. But they also recognize that there are limitations in the extent to which concepts of structure and hierarchy can be discarded and the extent to which it can be assumed that every job is going to be a joy. We have come to understand that a solidly based human relations approach to administration is or can be effective. But we have also come to recognize that human relations is not the end or purpose of administration. It is entirely possible, for example, to have a university in which the faculty have a satisfactory work environment where they participate with the administration in decision processes, where morale is high, and productivity is good. Despite all the best elements of the human relations approach, there will be squabbles over who gets what amount of pay, who has what titles, who is to receive tenure, and so on. And the human relations approach can be applied in such a way as to leave out a critical variable—"service recipient." The university may apply good human relations approaches and techniques to its faculty, but it may not provide services even approximating what the students want. And if it is a public university there may be a fundamental question of what the citizens or the board of trustees want.

Basically, the issue here is one of how the public servant defines the job to be done. If that job is defined as primarily the care and feeding of a particular bureaucracy, then human relations approaches are necessary. But, though necessary, they are not sufficient, at least sufficient to the maintenance of good government. The care and feeding of a university, or the care and feeding of a police department, or of any other public sector organization may not enable the organization to determine what the citizens expect of the organization. And the exclusive use of the human relations approach may exaggerate what the public service professionals intend to provide in the way of services. As a best guess, we are likely to see more middle- and upper-level public administrators working less within the organization and more with boundary problems, that is, relations between organizations and with clientele. This will result in part because of the demands of the citizens as they exercise the right to participate in public sector decisions that affect the services they receive. But it will also come about because of the manner or style that we are most likely to see in the next generation of public servants.

A corollary will be the much wider acceptance of and accommodation to environmental conflict. We grow to expect, understand, and work with conflict within the organization, and we develop routines for dealing with that conflict. It is more difficult for public servants to handle conflict at the borders of the organization. It is increasingly understood, however, that conflict at the borders is an ordinary and, indeed, desirable state of affairs and that effective public administrators accommodate rapidly to it, learn to receive and digest it, and assist their organizations in accommodating to it. This puts the organization in the position of confronting the citizen, knowing full well that citizens may not be in agreement with either the volume or the character of the organization's services. Nonetheless, confrontation is necessary. Transitory patterns of consensus will emerge and should be capitalized upon. Strong consensus extended through time, however, can be dangerous, because it may be nothing more than the expression of "majority rule." Although majority rule is fundamental to democratic principles, it is also clear that minority rights can thereby be threatened.

This should serve to indicate that the future of management-worker and management-citizen relations does not assume that the maintenance of a democratic system ends at the ballot box. Indeed, it assumes just the reverse—that the public administrator's job begins at the ballot box and that the completely effective public administrator has systems and procedures for routine interaction with citizens. As stated earlier, the best guess is that this will go well beyond the cosmetic procedures that we now see about us, such as ombudsmen and citizen's advisory councils. A summary of these views on management-worker, management-citizen relations is given in Table 5.

Table 5. Management-Worker, Management-Citizen Relations in New Public Administration

From	Transition	To
Authority from the top down.	Authority from the group.	Authority in the group.
Job as subsistence.	Job as high subsistence.	Job as satisfactory experience.
Regimented work environment.	Consultative work environment.	Democratic work environment.
Manage the "inside" of an organization well and it will be possible to have effective external relations (emphasize the internal).*	Deal with boundary relations by public relations techniques. Tell all how well the organization is doing.	Manage the boundary relations of an organization well and it will be possible to have effective internal arrangements (emphasize the environmental). Scan the boundary to see how the organization is doing.
Conflict should be avoided.*	Conflict is natural and must be expected.	Conflict is good, should be accommodated and used.
Consensus is necessary and confrontation may be tolerable (as long as it is transient). Confrontation may be productive of catastrophe if allowed to extend beyond marginal questions.*	Confrontation is good but must be managed so as to avoid displacing consensus.	Confrontation is necessary and consensus is tolerable (as long as a great premium is not placed upon it). Consensus may be productive of error if allowed to extend beyond the original conditions that produced it.

*Indicates a statement from Robert J. Biller, "Converting Knowledge into Action: Toward a Postindustrial Society," in Jong S. Jun and William B. Storm, eds., *Tomorrow's Organizations: Challenges and Strategies* (Glenville, Ill.: Scott, Foresman, 1973).

Summary and Conclusions

In the statics and dynamics of tomorrow's public administration we will be dealing with an accelerated process of change. The rapidity of change will force us to articulate and agree to change procedures and criteria and let these procedures and criteria represent stability in the public sector (rather than offices, titles, and the like). We will be forced to learn and relearn the difference between growth and change and will learn to be better managers of change and, particularly, decline as a form of change. Our leaders will come to be specialists in organizational adaption to citizens' needs and concerns and will gradually rely less on science and technology as the primary force for organizational or social change.

All of these changes will result in a serious criticism of our "rational" assumptions in public administration. We will be less heroic in our assumptions of what public administration can and cannot do. We will take more of an interest in understanding and rationalizing our activities and how they relate to goals and will focus less on ordering goals. There will be an increased questioning of what we are doing in public administration and why. Our certainty, our knowledge, and our wisdom will be seriously challenged, especially when seriously at odds with citizens' needs or expectations.

Finally, we will see the continued growth of human relations skills, group decision making, and organizational democracy. This will, however, be buffered by citizen involvement in organizational decision processes. We will gradually come to define the organization to include citizens, clients, elected officials, and the like. Good public managers now define their organizations in this very broad fashion.

5: The Geography of Public Administration

(6:30 a.m. My wife, sleepily) "Hello? You
want to speak to the Mayor? Well, it's awfully
early in the. . . . All right, just a minute.
(Poking me) Hey! Psst! It's for you, Highness."
  (Early morning bass) "This is the Mayor speaking."
  "Mayor?"
  "Yes. Who is this?"
  "This is a taaaaaxpayer."
  "What can I do for you?"
  "Mayor. I seen that big pitchur in the paper last
night about redoin' the whole East Side—tearin' down
all those tenements and puttin' up a new civic center.
That your idea?"
  (A little proudly) "Why, yes."
  "Mayor."
  "Yes."
  "Why the hell don't you stop tryin' to build Radio
City and come down here and collect my garbage. It
stinks!" (Click!)—Stephen K. Bailey, "A Structured
Interaction Pattern for Harpsichord and Kazoo"

Orthodoxy

The earliest attempts to comprehend organizations in this
century were structural. Max Weber designed a formal
model based on a hierarchy of authority—a hierarchy that
was unidimensionally mapped (by others) on a piece of
paper.[1] Thus began the organization chart. In attempting
either to describe how the organization works or to design
the workings of an ideal organization, the classic organization scholars gave much of their attention to the boxes and
to the solid and dotted lines of the organization chart. A
distribution was made during this era between the functional
or line hierarchy on the one hand and the auxiliary staff
hierarchy on the other, as well as between the auxiliary staff

and the advisory staff. And during this time the search began for the most efficient and economical design for the "engine" we called organization.

As organizations grew more complex, organization charts became more elaborate. Political parties already had developed wards and precincts, and bureaus began to establish field offices; thus the concept of "decentralization" was born. Administrative decentralization made it necessary to decide how to treat auxiliary staff services such as budgeting, personnel, and purchasing. Should the head of a geographically separate subunit of the organization control the auxiliary staff people in his office, or should they report directly to their counterpart specialists at the bureau headquarters? Depending on the situation, one answer was probably as good as another, despite the "principles" developed by early theorists to answer each question in the abstract. What was clear was the extreme difficulty of dealing with such structural questions abstractly or of mapping such complexities on a flat sheet of paper.

As the organization grew, it became apparent that not all decisions could be made at the top. Questions were raised about the merits of centralization versus decentralization and about which was better for what kinds of administrative activities. Rapid increases in organizational size and complexity resulted not only in decentralization, but also in an emphasis on both the line item budget to ensure accountability and the position classifications and elaborate task descriptions to improve the manager's capacity to control the organization. And in all of this a new specialization, or skill, or perhaps even science seemed to be emerging—the science of management or administration.

Management scientists were especially prominent in industry during the first two decades of the twentieth century. Because of the capacity of industry to produce great quantities of consumable items, there developed a widespread belief that industrial organization was the most efficient means to accomplish any goal. This led to a wholesale transfer of the management sciences into the public sector.

The city manager plan is an organizational design borrowed basically from a simplistic concept of the corporation. Budgeting and personnel systems were widely adopted in government largely from business and industry during the reform era. Much of the spirit as well as the concepts behind the reform movement in government concerned attempts to bring about more efficient, economical organizational designs. Borrowed from industry, these attempts include merit concepts, line-item budgets, the elimination of "politics" from organization, the development of the policy-administration dichotomy, and particularly the use of auxiliary staff services as control techniques by public managers. Indeed, the early concepts of a bureau of the budget were based on a need to strengthen the administration and management of public affairs and at least implicitly to strengthen the hand of the president, the governor, or the mayor as the counterpart of the corporation president.

For several reasons, the structural emphasis in early public administration has stayed with us. First, closely connected with early management science, it is considered scientific. Second, the success of the reform movement has greatly strengthened the administrative apparatus in many governments throughout the land. Third, many of the procedures and techniques established in early public administration have continued as traditions, such as elaborate position descriptions and classifications, or the formalization of positions and responsibilities by organizational charts that must be signed by bureau chiefs or secretaries of cabinet level departments in the national government. And fourth, there has been a preoccupation in American government with organizations based on simple models of hierarchy, with little propensity to explore other organizational structures. Organization has come to mean hierarchy.

The Fall from Orthodoxy

The critics of this orthodoxy, however, raised several cogent points. The approach to organization is vastly too mechanistic. It considered one individual as roughly similar to another, and, as such, the individual became an interchangeable part in the organization. The resulting view, then, was of the organization as a machine, requiring an ample supply of parts in order to work effectively. Thus, the efficiency of the administrative engine was stressed to the point of ignoring the importance and dignity of the individual.

Critics further noted that the organization chart did not seem to represent organizational behavior. They pointed out that there really was no science of management and that, in fact, it was impossible to find a "span of control" that was ideal or to design an organization that did not violate the principle of "unity of command." Moreover, critics maintained, the preoccupation with structure and administration had a stifling effect on the individual, making him feel insignificant, a "personnel" rather than a "person," generally oppressed by insensitive and aloof administrators up that formal and hated hierarchy.

Beginning with the Hawthorne experiments in the late 1920s, there emerged a new direction in the study of administration.[2] The informal organization was discovered, and most students of administration have been preoccupied with it ever since. This new generation of administrative theorists wanted to know how the organization worked, for they were interested primarily in building a body of theory that would account for organizational behavior. The "human relations school" of administration, composed primarily of sociologists, social psychologists, and psychologists, became increasingly important in the study of administration. The focus was first on the individual, his needs, his motives, and his role; second, on the work group, its positive and negative sanctions and the manner in which it constituted a "natural" hierarchy. And it was the general view at this time that the formal design of organizations was either unimportant or simply an impediment to the working of the informal organization.

From the human relations school emerged the current strong interest in sensitivity training, now more commonly known as organizational development. Organizational development is an applied version of group dynamics or modern organizational psychology. Generally, it is an attempt to unfreeze the organization. The emphasis is on thawing the coolness that accompanies status differences in the formal hierarchy and on developing levels of trust and openness not common in hierarchies. The purpose of organizational development is to enhance the dignity of the individual in the organization, to develop high levels of empathy among individuals, to develop cohesiveness, to reduce preoccupation with status competition, to allow the individual to find that place in the organization where he feels most suited, and to nurture open and honest communications within the organization and between the organization and its clientele. The adherents to the human relations school and its child, the organizational development movement, are explicitly value conscious about what is "good and bad" in organizations. In this normative framework, hierarchy is bad; "natural structure" is good.[3]

But as time passes it becomes increasingly clear that the human relations perspective on organization is not nirvana. Any impact it has made on organizational behavior is at the supervisory level, where it is increasingly clear that "authoritarian" styles of supervision result in both lower production and fewer feelings of worker satisfaction than do "democratic" styles of supervision.[4]

Still, these limitations have had little impact on the workings of complex organizations, particularly publicly administered organizations. The more modern version of sensitivity training—organizational development—has been challenged by one of its most prominent spokesmen, Warren Bennis, who feels that until the structure of organizations is truly decentralized, organizational development will never be effective.[5]

It is also increasingly clear that the preoccupation of the human relations perspective with the care and feeding of the internal organization has done little for the organization's clients. Those who must receive services from public bureaucracies or buy the products and services of industrial bureaucracies are less and less satisfied with the quality and equity of these services and products. Even if the organization is in better health internally (which some would doubt), it is patently clear that the clients of organizations are paying the price.

Thus, in a time of discontinuity and temporariness we search for means by which large-scale organizations can be made both more responsive to all their clients and more conducive to human growth.[6] This search leads to a fundamental reconsideration of organizational structure, for only with changed structures can the aims of the human relations perspective be achieved.

The non-human-relations outgrowth of the fall from orthodoxy appears most particularly in the writings published in the *Administrative Science Quarterly*. Unlike the organizational development movement, there is little emphasis in this journal on attempts to improve or change organizations. Rather, adherents to the "administrative science" perspective focus on building a theory that best explains the manner in which organizations operate. Their approach is only implicitly value conscious, accepting the norms of science and the presumption that if organizations were better understood they could be better managed, controlled, or changed. Scholars of this persuasion therefore have not customarily taken a strong interest in formal organization. As a result, organizational structure has been too long neglected.

The Search for a New Orthodoxy

We now see more clearly that the organizational rules of the game are set through formal structure. The organizational structure is the framework, or mask, for substantive indications of individual or group status, power, skills, and effectiveness. And the mask determines in part all of these things.

Recent research indicates that in the United States the formal design of city government is an important factor in its output. Cities with the manager plan, nonpartisan elections, and full merit systems tend to have policy outcomes that differ from cities with other structures.[7] As the detailed research of the fluoridation controversy in many localities in the United States indicates, for example, the structure of government is also fundamental to its response to public policy issues.[8]

As we try to improve the effectiveness of organizations (a shift from our preoccupation with understanding them), the restructuring of these organizations captures our interest. The assumption implicit in the human relations perspective was that if one could change the people in the organization, the organization would be changed. I am arguing, with Bennis, that changing the people will come to naught unless the organization is redesigned.

The recovery of interest in organizational structure has come about for three reasons. First, organization theorists, who were once content to explain how organizations work, are now interested in change. When organizations are working well, we seem to understand them. But now organizations, both public and private, are not working well. Indeed, they are under severe criticism, so we seek to change them. From the above agreement we can derive this hypothesis: As the interest in organizational change rises, the interest in organizational structure also rises. Following this hypothesis is this premise: "It is easier to change the design of organizations and thereby the rules of the game than it is to change the people, and by changing the design and rules we can enhance the potential for changing the people."

Second, the simple hierarchy does not seem to accommodate effectively the increased complexity of our society. Both theorists and managers are asking themselves if it is at all sensible to conceptualize as a hierarchy an organization the size of the Defense Department. Defense is just too big and too complex for such a concept, yet we have no concept to replace hierarchy. Clearly, we need more sophisticated means by which to describe existing organizations as well as to design new and better ones.

Third, organizations appear to become increasingly isolated from and indifferent to their clients. As Herbert Kaufman has indicated, we are moving from a primary concern for internal administrative effectiveness to a basic concern for responsiveness.[9] The mood that argues for responsiveness is born out of the frustrations of attempting to get from complex public organizations the level of services to which the citizen feels he is entitled. The recovery of interest in organizational structure derives, then, from the demand for client responsiveness, the need for an accommodation to the complexity of our world, and the need for change. Five structural models are suggested here, which meet in varying degrees the demands described above: (1) the administrative decentralization model, (2) the neighborhood control model, (3) the matrix model, (4) the federated model, and (5) the bargaining model.

The Administrative Decentralization Model

Frank Sherwood and John Pfiffner once noted that there was a "gospel of decentralization" in administrative organizations.[10] The successful General Motors format was widely hailed and often copied. Proposals for federal decentralization have been developed by Dwight Ink and others.[11] Richard Nixon, while president, developed the "New Federalism" with expanded federal field offices, revenue sharing, and the like. Still, it is probably safe to say that we speak decentralization and act centralization. We have read the decentralization gospel, but we have difficulty living it. Why?

The first reason is that true administrative decentralization is a severe modification of hierarchy because it allows substantial autonomy for each subunit in the structure. Such autonomy can result in differing standards and procedures in the semiautonomous subunits of the organization. Few organizations and fewer administrators are sufficiently mature to be tolerant of such differences. True administrative decentralization requires a real delegation of power, and most administrators find it difficult to delegate.[12]

Yet the decentralization rhetoric, the gospel, is compelling. The decentralized organization supports the growth of individuals lower in the hierarchy by expanding their real responsibilities: it provides a training ground for top-level management; it furthers individual incentive; and it allows enough autonomy to enable each subunit to adjust to the special needs of its own clientele and environment.

The second main reason why we do not live decentralization is because of some possible negative consequences. The U.S. Selective Service System was geographically and administratively decentralized, as are many of the bureaus of the U.S. Department of Agriculture. Both the local draft boards and the local agents of Agriculture were controlled by local elites and tend to reflect segregation in the South, the interests of big farmers over small farmers, the interests of local industrialists and managers over local laboring people, and the like.[13] We see another version of the problem in our federal system of government, a true geographic and political decentralization. The federal system has been a constant struggle between states' rights, used to suppress racial minorities, and federal power, used to enforce "human rights" laws.[14]

The most elaborate characterization of decentralization is Larry Kirkhart's consociated model, derived basically from organization development thinking and from a branch of social philosophy and from phenomenology. The consociated model has the following characteristics: (1) Basic work unit is a project team. (2) Hierarchy is nonpermanent and leadership is situational. (3) Strict time limitations are imposed on all that is done. (4) Diverse projects work on the same problem or goal. (5) There is high interpersonnel competence and trust. (6) Clients to be served are represented in the organization. (7) Organization is a place of employment, not necessarily a career. (8) Record keeping is computer based. (9) Funds are allocated on a program basis.[15]

Kirkhart's model is a rather complete modification of the classic hierarchy. It resembles in many ways the kind of organization urged by Warren Bennis, who suggests that organizations must be truly decentralized and must devolve into a state of "organic populism."[16] "Organic" is taken to mean "natural" rather than the imposed condition of the classic hierarchy. "Populism" is taken to mean "emerging to meet the basic needs of the organization's clients." But to both Bennis and Kirkhart, the principal concern is for the internal workings of the organization rather than for the welfare of the clients of that organization.

One of the nation's foremost social scientists, Rensis Likert, has done extensive research on work group behavior as it relates to organizational design. He found close correlation between worker satisfaction and worker productivity.[17] Like Bennis, he attaches great importance to the design or geography of an organization. Based on research, he recommends an organizational design with "overlapping work groups" with key people who serve a "linking pin function." The overlapping work group is illustrated by Figure 1, taken from Likert. Note that the supervisor of one level is a member of the work group at the next level, serving a linking pin—or upward influence—function.

Figure 1. The Overlapping Work Group and Linking Pin Function

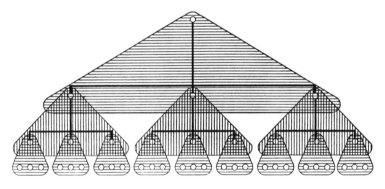

The overlapping group form of organization. Work groups vary in size as circumstances require although shown here as consisting of four persons. Adapted from Rensis Likert, *New Patterns of Management* (New York: McGraw-Hill Book Company, Inc., 1961), p. 105.

In later research, Likert illustrated the role of a subordinate in horizontal coordination, as shown in Figure 2.[18]

Figure 2. The Subordinate as Linking Pin

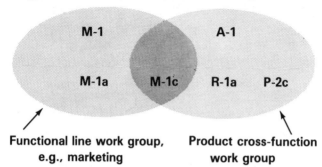

Adapted from Rensis Likert, *The Human Organization* (New York: McGraw-Hill Book Company, Inc., 1967), p. 160.

Finally, Likert shows a vertical group linkage model that comprehends a "family" or more than one person in a vertical linking role (see Figure 3). He also illustrates in a model, not shown here, a combination of vertical and horizontal overlapping work groups and linking pin functions. For such models to work he insists that the whole organization must use multiple overlapping group structures and must be effective in group decision-making processes.

The Neighborhood Control Model

Similar in many respects to the decentralized model is the neighborhood control model. Neighborhood control has to do particularly with government or public organizations and is therefore less widely applicable than the administrative decentralization model. Neighborhood control suggests that a collectivity of citizens has the power to decide the kinds and levels of services their government(s) should provide. Clearly, the best available example of this model is the suburban municipality that provides the school systems, trash collection, parks and recreation services, and law enforcement its residents want. Neighborhood control argues that those who live in huge central cities should be entitled to no less than those who live in autonomous suburbs.[19]

Figure 3. Multiple, Overlapping Group Structures

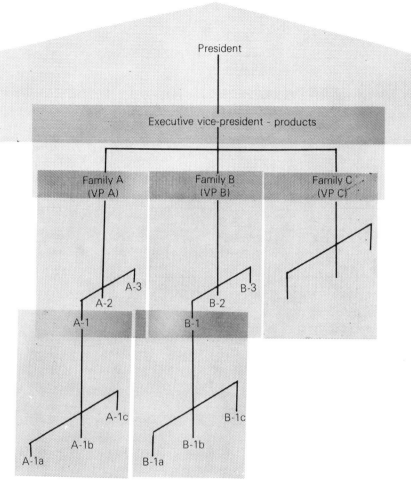

Adapted from Rensis Likert, *The Human Organization* (New York: McGraw-Hill Book Company, Inc., 1967), p. 166.

During the era of American government when the police precinct and political ward were in full flower, there was a form of neighborhood control. Since that time, we have professionalized and centralized our police systems, our education systems, and even to some extent our political parties. As a consequence, the people who live in the neighborhoods of our great cities increasingly feel that the public bureaucracies are not sensitive to their peculiar and unique needs. The people in the neighborhood, particularly blacks, Puerto Ricans, and Mexican-Americans, want control over those institutions that most directly affect their lives.

The three most complete models of neighborhood control are taken from George Frederickson, Milton Kotler, and Charles Benson and Peter Lund.[20] All three models are a clear reflection of Bennis's argument that even if the organization is administratively decentralized, it may not be responsive to the needs of its varied clientele. The neighborhood control model, designed to meet both client and organizational needs, has the following characteristics. (1) The residents of the neighborhood decide, with organizational representatives, the level and types of services wanted, and they share control of personnel and management decisions in the organization. (2) The level and type of services varies from neighborhood to neighborhood. (3) Some services might be offered by neighborhood-owned corporations or by privately owned contractors. (4) The neighborhood is defined where possible on the basis of economic and social homogeneity. (5) The central city and the wider metropolitan area continue to serve as the tax base, and allocations to the neighborhood are made on a per capita plus need basis. Once the funds are allocated, they are controlled by the neighborhood.

The Matrix Model

The matrix model of organization structure is an attempt to deal with the organization's resistance to change and its concentration on self-survival. Its name is derived from the type of chart used to illustrate it (see Figures 4 and 5). The first argument in the matrix model is for the "project approach." Opposed to the view that the major tasks of an organization are fixed and eternal, the matrix model proposed that the organization's energies should be directed toward projects that are, by definition, temporary, with a definite date for completion and with considerable latitude in their budgets, personnel, and management matters.[21] When a project is finished, the organization can then decide if it wants to repeat it and, if so, in what ways. The role of the project manager in a matrix format is to get the job done, not to make his part of the organization everlasting. Rewards are based upon successful job completion, not upon the building of organization. Indeed, the project manager has recently been described as "someone who does what he said he would."

The best examples of matrix organization are the National Aeronautics and Space Administration and those parts of government doing extensive capital development on a project basis. In both cases, the product of the organization, such as a building or a rocket, is tangible and "built." By using a matrix format an organization like NASA can at one point in time have a six-billion-dollar budget, which, within five to seven years, can be reduced to half that size and can, we presume, expand or contract along with interest in space exploration.

For the matrix model to work, there must be consistent support from top-level management for the needs and interests of the projects over those of the permanent, or support, part of the organization. The purchasing department, the budgeting department, the personnel department, and all the other permanent staff agencies must bend to the needs and concerns of the projects so that they may be completed well and on time. Personnel rules are not kept for the sake of keeping them, but, according to the recommendations of the project manager, are kept if they make sense and broken if they do not. Budgeting tends to be a package or program variety; the project is allotted a certain sum of money to complete its responsibilities, with less stringent authorizations for salaries and materials than in a nonmatrix format. A simple model of the matrix format is shown in Figure 4.

The critical points in this model are the "nodes" connecting the projects and the staff agencies. These nodes require

Figure 4. A Simple Model of the Matrix Format

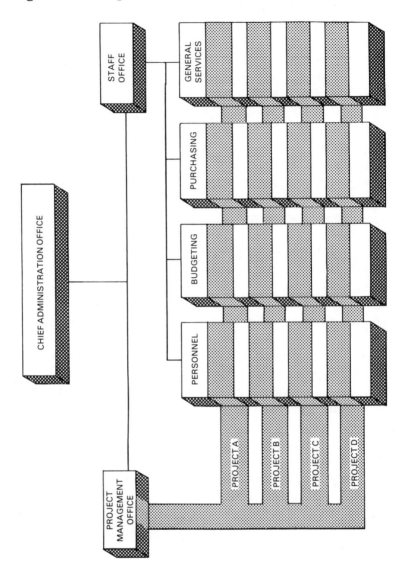

persons who can cope with ambiguity and who can focus and sharpen the preferences of different groups so as to keep communications open and enhance the potential for decisions and policies that further the completion of the job well and on time.

A more complex matrix format is illustrated in Figure 5. This figure shows greater complexity by indicating the points at which a project intersects a department and a staff service. If a city had geographic subdivisions such as a "little city hall" system or some modified form of neighborhood control, the projects shown in Figure 5 could represent these geographic subdivisions. Obviously, a cubic design such as Figure 5 could illustrate six rather than three sides to each point of interaction (cube or node). Such designs are especially useful in graphically describing the real complexity of large-scale public organizations. They further illustrate the ambiguity and the interrelatedness of modern organizations. For example, a glance at Figure 5 should indicate that many public employees have several "bosses" to whom their responsibilities are neither certain nor clear-cut. This ambiguity, which is very common in modern organizations, is not conveyed by the simple hierarchical-based organization chart. Further, Figure 5 shows that actions taken in a department affect a project and staff service, an illustration of interrelatedness.

There is little question that the matrix approach is effective in reducing the organizational tendency to expend vast sums of money and time on survival. It seems an ideal model for a time when our society is increasingly inclined to high mobility and temporariness. The ease with which engineers move from project to project and job to job might serve as an excellent example for those public organizations suffering from common rigidities and permanence. There is some question, though, as to the applicability of the matrix format to those kinds of public enterprises that are essentially services. Is it possible, for instance, to have a project format in a social service agency or in the post office? For some government functions the model is clearly inapplicable, but

Figure 5. A More Complex Model of the Matrix Format

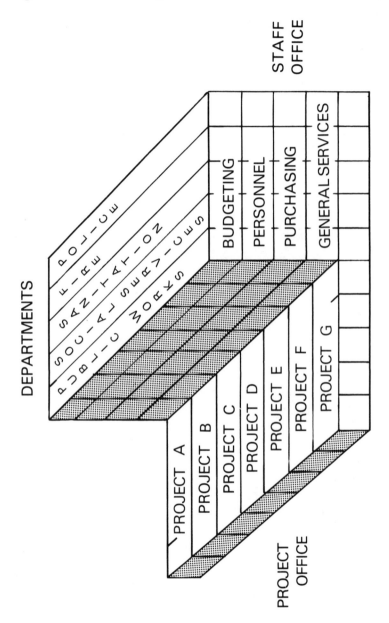

for others, particularly in local government and in education and within the large departments of the national government, such as Agriculture, the model may be usable.

The Federated Model

The federated model can accommodate both decentralization and neighborhood control. The most thorough description of a federated model as applied to metropolitan areas can be found in a publication of the Council for Economic Development, *Reshaping Government in Metropolitan Areas.*[22] The Council suggests the following as the salient characteristics of the federated metropolitan model:

1. Metropolitan government should have two tiers.
   a. Planning, transportation and water, air and sewerage activities would be totally centralized.
   b. Other local functions have both centralized and decentralized characteristics. For rubbish and garbage collection, police, health, housing, and welfare, the neighborhood would have much more control than it now does over the manner in which the service is delivered. Record keeping, general policy, relations to the state and national governments, and the like would be more centralized than they now are.
2. The county (or counties) would assume the centralized responsibilities.
3. Cities, suburban towns, subdivisions of cities (neighborhood government), and the like would assume decentralized responsibilities.
4. Finance would be area wide, with more equitable state and federal aid and a more equitable distribution of resources between the subunits in the metropolitan area.

The Bargaining Model

The bargaining model derives initially from studies of contracting between units of governments in southern California under what has come to be known as the Lakewood Plan. In a bargaining format, one unit of government can provide services to another unit of government, or the governments can go to the private sector for services, or they can employ any useful combination. In short, the bargaining model argues that governments should be as imaginative and creative as possible in providing services. Establishing a permanent civil service may not be the most efficient way to provide services.

The bargaining model, at least as it has been set out by Vincent Ostrom, Charles Tiebout, and Robert Warren, argues that taking all the units of government in a particular metropolitan area and amalgamating them into one large "metro" would be counterproductive.[23] According to the bargaining format, it is more useful to continue the present jurisdictions and establish numerous special district governments; to encourage the exchange of personnel among these governments; to increase the capacity of these governments to contract with one another; and by other means to allow each government its own pattern of preferred relationships with all the governments around it. In this way, if an areawide problem exists, a special district government can be created to cope with that problem. Once that problem is effectively dealt with, that special district government can be moved to a stable pattern rather than a growth pattern. The best examples of such special districts are in environmental pollution and flood control. Other services that are more traditionally local, such as schools, law enforcement, and health care, can be provided in any combination of ways, depending on the preferences of any particular jurisdiction.

A small area may incorporate and contract for all of its services with a county government and negotiate these contracts annually, thereby improving the character and quality of service. In this way, the city avoids erecting its own elaborate organization and has, instead, two or three brokers who negotiate and monitor service contracts. Similarly, large cities may subdivide for particular services but continue to offer those services to the neighborhood subdivisions on a contract basis, allowing those in the neighborhood subdivisions to stipulate the manner they wish the services delivered. In this way, a form of neighborhood control can be developed. In sum, then, the bargaining model applies marketing logic to the public sector and stands as an alternative to a single areawide organization providing all services through a large hierarchy.

Toward Structural Dynamics in Public Administration

These models, and variations of them, are not mere theory, for they describe organizations that now exist in most metropolitan areas in the nation. For example, in Los Angeles County, the following structural arrangements are found. In the City of Los Angeles, administrative decentralization functions through branch city halls whereby district superintendents make limited decisions for outlying communities. Some branch city halls provide the complete services of the main city hall. Neighborhood control is provided through the community corporations of the community action program. Neighborhood residents as well as the mayor and councilmen are represented on the central policy-making board. The matrix concept is found in the temporary projects of the neighborhood youth corps, summer recreation programs, demonstration food programs, head start experiments, urban renewal projects, and the like. The federated concept is exemplified by the division of services between Los Angeles County, which performs broader area programs, such as air pollution, water and sewerage, welfare, certain tax collections, and the like, and the city of Los Angeles and the other municipalities, which perform localized pollution inspections, neighborhood social service and food programs, and many regular city government services, such as police and fire protection. The bargaining model is used in an elaborate set of contractual relationships between the county government and municipalities. Contracts can provide for all local services or any selected combination of them depending on the needs of the municipality. The contracts are, of course, terminal.

From this description, it is apparent that these models are not mutually exclusive; rather, they all work at the same time in the same metropolitan area. An experienced urban administrator is likely to recognize these models because they are in common use. These structural complexities are not, however, reflected in the literature of public administration, which has remained more or less on the hierarchy model. This disparity between what we "know" and what we, as theorists, have been able to describe or explain is commonplace.

To remedy this discrepancy we must first recognize that organizational structure is not static; it is changing and changeable. Second, we must see that the complexity of modern public organizations cannot be fully comprehended by the hierarchy concept. We suggest that the models that have been presented, and other structural models, be subsumed under the phrase "structural dynamics," which indicates that structures are not fixed and not necessarily hierarchical. The phrase further indicates that theory or knowledge about structural alternatives is important. To follow the hypothesis presented earlier in this essay, structural approaches to organization change are sorely needed.

The forces behind the renewed interest in structure can be traced to (1) the strongly felt need to change our hierarchy-based publicly administered organizations, because they are simply no longer effective; (2) a fresh concern for responsiveness to the needs of clients; and (3) a need for better ways of accommodating to the complexity, temporariness, and discontinuity of our time. Taken alone, none of the five models presented above appears to meet all three of these factors and respond to all situations.

Decentralization and neighborhood control break down the hierarchy and greatly enhance responsiveness; however, decentralized neighborhood government may become fixed and rigid, unable to accommodate to future changes. The matrix model is ideally designed for temporariness and change, but seems difficult to apply to certain kinds of public services. The bargaining model can be regarded as an apology for things as they now are, but in theory at least, a bargaining format can accommodate decentralization of large governments and neighborhood control. Moreover, the contracting strategy, as used in both the matrix model and the bargaining model, enhances the capacity to make organizations changeable. Of the five models, the federated approach comes the closest to being a grand framework in which any of the other four models can operate.

Organization structure is crucially important, but its importance should not be exaggerated. Such exaggeration in early public administration resulted in a reaction so that for

Table 6. Structure in the New Public Administration

From	Transition	To
Centralization helps the manager make and effectuate the right decision.*	Some decentralization may help the manager know how right his decision is.	Decentralize—the task of the manager is to make sure that good decisions get made in the bowels of the organization and to be certain that they are not blocked.
Hierarchy	Social process	Small decentralized hierarchies with large terminal projects.
Develop the people in organizations by sensitivity training, responsibility expansion, etc.	Develop the organization by keeping present structure but changing all the people. Organizational development.	Undevelop the organization by dividing it into autonomous units of changed people.

*Indicates a statement from Robert J. Biller, "Converting Knowledge into Action: Toward a Postindustrial Society," in Jong S. Jun and William B. Storm, eds., *Tomorrow's Organizations: Challenges and Strategies* (Glenville, Ill.: Scott, Foresman, 1973).

a long period questions of organization structure were disregarded. The workings of the informal organization, group behavior, individual behavior, the pattern of power and communication, will always modify hierarchies or any other structures. We can now develop models that serve as the designs for future organizations, informed by all that we now know about the informal organization. But we must also turn to structural dynamics, for it is apparent that publicly administered organizations are being overhauled and redesigned. As this happens, knowledge should guide change.

6: Education and Public Administration

The universities offer the best hope
for making the professions safe
for democracy.—Frederick C. Mosher,
Democracy and the Public Service

New public administration is closely associated with education, and no aspect of public administration has shown more change and development than education. Indeed, education for public administration is almost completely new. This is not because education has been ahead of practice, but mostly because it has begun to catch up. As is usually the case with many applied fields such as public administration, theory becomes the synthesis and articulation of practice. Such is certainly the case in public administration. There are dramatic changes in the size and type of education programs for public administration. There are changes in public administration pedagogy. There are changes in the quantity level and character of government employment. And we are entering an era of even greater change in public administration education.

Public Administration Education—Size, Type, Structure

Higher education in the United States has stabilized in terms of both enrollment and resources in the last decade. Enrollments grow only gradually, and annual increments in dollars have been less than the rate of inflation. We have passed the great era of growth in higher education. In this period of education stability, public administration is one of the most rapidly growing fields. Twenty years ago, approximately 30 institutions in the United States gave graduate degrees (usually M.P.A.). In 1972, 108 schools offered such degrees, and in 1978 there were approximately 200 programs in public administration. Enrollment in 1972 was 6,150 students full time and 6,450 students part time, for a total of 12,600 students. By 1976, that enrollment had almost doubled. Such growth in a period of general quiescence in higher education is phenomenal. It has also resulted in some important questions and dilemmas, both for those who are engaged in public service education and for those responsible for the management of government affairs. Some of these questions are as follows: How are public administration programs organized? What employment characteristics and conditions should be considered in the development of curricula for public service education? What underlying theoretical or epistomological premises have, or ought, to guide public administration pedagogy? And what ought to be the relationship between public administration programs and the rest of higher education?

Organization for Public Service Education

There can be little question that political science is the mother discipline for public administration education. Almost all the early scholars in public administration were political scientists (Wilson, White, Goodnow, Willoughby, Pfiffner). Present-day organizational patterns for public service education are to some extent a manifestation of that lineage. Approximately one-third of all M.P.A. degree programs are given by or within political science departments.

There are a variety of ways of evaluating that arrangement, and any evaluation will of course be judgmental. One of the more generous analyses of this arrangement is done by Richard Chapman and Frederic N. Cleaveland in their report *Meeting the Needs of Tomorrow's Public Service: Guidelines for Professional Education in Public Administration*:

> Usually, although not universally, the research of faculty teaching in the public administration program tends to be of a more applied nature, and less applicable as academic

research. This tends also to apply to the important related functions of continuing, non-degree education and consulting services for which public administration faculty frequently are called upon. In the faculty "pecking order" these activities are judged to be of lesser importance, and tend to put those affiliated with a public administration program at a general disadvantage in the faculty and university rewards system. In addition, except where public administration programs have been initiated and supported by the leadership of the department, the public administration faculty tend to be a small minority in the department, frequently outvoted when it comes to budget questions, and the assignment of new positions.[1]

This is not to suggest that the M.P.A. degree given out of political science departments is per force improperly organized, but only to point up the problems associated with that pattern of organization.

A less generous analysis of the situation can be found in a compilation of data done by Alice and Donald Stone. The Stones trace the evolution of M.P.A. programs and point out that almost all of the early degree programs were vest pocket operations in political science departments. Many universities in the United States had distinguished faculty in public administration in the 1920s and 1930s and relatively vigorous programs in the field. These include the University of California–Berkeley, Stanford University, Syracuse University, University of Cincinnati, University of Wisconsin, University of Southern California, University of Minnesota, Columbia University, University of Chicago, and University of Michigan. Only the public administration programs at Syracuse and Southern California survived and still are vigorous. Berkeley, Michigan, and Minnesota have recently rediscovered public administration and organized full schools of public policy or public affairs. Each of these programs is now established in a separate and autonomous school of public affairs, whereas the programs at the other universities have disappeared or are considerably less distinguished and rather more regional in scope. The Stones conclude that the manner in which a public administration program is organized in a university is critical to its longevity and that such programs in political science departments tend to be vulnerable.[2]

A couple of trends are discernible here. First, several M.P.A. programs that have traditionally been affiliated with political science departments have become autonomous either as schools or departments of public administration. The new School of Public Policy at Berkeley, the School of Public Affairs at Minnesota, the School of Public Affairs at Arizona State, the School of Public and Environmental Affairs at Indiana, the Division of Urban Affairs at Delaware, the Graduate School of Public Affairs at Colorado, and several others have chosen this alternative. Second, many new M.P.A. programs have developed within political science departments at universities previously offering no program in the field. This seems to indicate, at the very least, that political science departments provide an excellent point for beginning public administration programs, but, over the long haul, they encounter difficulty sustaining such programs.

It is important to observe that there is a very strong shift in political science toward more applied subjects. The growth and vigor of the Policy Studies Organization and the sales of the *Policy Studies Journal* seem to indicate that increasing numbers of political scientists have taken an interest in policy-related subjects. This may indicate the likely development of even more public administration programs or at least policy studies or policy analysis programs in political science departments.

The second most common arrangement in a university for public affairs education is a separate school for public affairs. These schools range in size from a few faculty to eighty-five faculty members at the School of Public and Environmental Affairs at Indiana University. Among these schools are the major older schools with high stature in public administration, including the Maxwell School at Syracuse University, the School of Public Administration at the

University of Southern California, the Graduate School of International and Public Affairs at Pittsburgh, the School of Public Affairs at New York University, the School of Public Affairs at State University of New York at Albany, the Woodrow Wilson School at Princeton University, the John F. Kennedy School at Harvard, the School of Public Administration at American University, the Graduate School of Public Affairs at the University of Washington, and several others. All of these schools are now at least twenty years old and have a special place in public affairs education.

Several prestigious American universities have recently developed separate schools of public affairs, including Minnesota, Michigan, Arizona, Berkeley, Colorado, Indiana, Texas at Austin, Carnegie-Mellon, and Arizona State. It is interesting that the schools in this latter list are almost all products of the last decade, a presumed period of stagnation in higher education.

This arrangement is not without its problems, of course. First, a separate school of public administration can become as insular from the rest of the university as any other department or school. Becoming separate may have included burning bridges with departments of political science as well as other social science departments. Second, these schools are new in their universities and therefore must come from behind in the struggle for resources. Most of them, however, seem to have done relatively well to date. Third, bringing together an interdisciplinary faculty is always difficult. How these schools are staffed, that is, the ratio of faculty who are educated basically in public administration vis-à-vis faculty educated in the social sciences is a critical question.

Even with these problems, however, it appears that the development of schools of public affairs is one of the most important innovations in the last decade in American higher education.

The third most common arrangement for public service education is in combination with a business school. Several well-known programs in public administration are thus or-

ganized, including those at Cornell, University of Missouri–
Kansas City, University of California–Irvine, University of
California–Riverside, University of Arizona, Stanford University, Northwestern University, Ohio State, and Yale
University. Many of these schools are truly "generic"; that
is, they are relatively balanced between business and public
inclinations in the composition of the faculty and the student
body. Several schools of business with public administration
programs in them, however, have basically the same problem as public administration programs in political science
departments. The bulk of the students and the faculty are in
business administration, and the public administration program is a minor and relatively unimportant aspect of the
school.

In the last five years, schools of business have become
strongly interested in the public sector. Consequently, several of them have changed their names to schools of administration, management, or administrative sciences and have
developed either public sector concentrations in M.B.A.
programs or separate M.P.A. programs. Yale University's
new School of Administration gives the Master's of Public
and Private Management (M.P.P.M.). The more established
schools of business have been an entry point into the public
service for their graduates. This is particularly true of the
schools of business at Harvard and Chicago.

The premise, of course, is that management is the central
subject matter to be taught and that the student can adapt
these management skills to either public or private settings.
Although it is difficult to fault the logic of the generic school,
evidence indicates that there are serious problems of growth
and maturation for public administration education in such
settings. The appeal to educators of the generic school may
not be shared by their professional constituency. The generic school may be ignoring the fundamental difference
between the clientele of business administration as against
the clientele of public administration. One is from the world
of business and industry, the other from the world of government. It is logical to argue that management ought to be the
core of both the M.B.A. and the M.P.A. and that the

student can adapt to either the public or private setting. That logic, however, may wilt in the presence of the traditional support in the business community for schools of business. Corporations and businesses, who hire the bulk of M.B.A.s, are, I would argue, different from federal, state, and local government officials in their professional orientations and needs. The difficulty of trying to satisfy in one school and in one degree program the preferences of these two clienteles may have been underestimated.

One of the most interesting recent developments in public service education has to do with relationships between public administration and the other public service professions. Several newer schools bring together public service professions, such as criminal justice, urban and regional planning, social services administration, recreation and park administration, community development, and the like. There are many variations of this arrangement. The better known schools include the Lila Atchison Wallace School of Community and Public Service at the University of Oregon, the School of Community Services at the University of Cincinnati, and the School of Public and Community Services at the University of Massachusetts–Boston. At the University of Missouri, the Institute of Public Administration is campuswide, involving the Colleges of Arts and Sciences, Engineering, Medicine, Public and Community Services, and Business and Public Administration, being administered by the latter. These newer programs may be a way of getting at a fundamental problem long found in the practice of public administration—that is, that there really are several public service professions. Each profession is logically a separate department, school, or college in the university. John C. Honey's "Report" that appeared in 1967 urged ways of combining these programs, for example, under a provost or chancellor for public or community services. Several universities have such arrangements, including the University of Maryland and Duke University.

Another variation on this theme is the combination of degree programs. For example, it is now common to find the M.P.A. degree taken in combination with the J.D. Increasingly, one sees the M.P.A. taken in conjunction with the M.S.W. The most elaborate arrangement of this sort is the Institute of Policy Sciences and Public Affairs at Duke University. At Duke, the M.P.A. student must take the M.P.A. degree in conjunction with some other degree. There are now formal programs combining the M.P.A. with the M.D., the Doctorate of Divinity, the J.D., and the M.S.W.

It is important to remember that education for the public service in the United States is relatively new as an organized and self-conscious activity. It should not surprise us, then, that universities are organizing for it in a variety of ways. There simply is no standard or universally accepted format. At this point, it would be foolhardy to argue that one approach is better than another. Each university should be encouraged to organize as it prefers. But it should be added that each university should be encouraged to support whatever arrangement it chooses for public service education. What should be clear and obvious is that education for the public service has come of age and that most major universities have formalized programs for this purpose. Maturation in public service education may well result in a fairly standard format at the university. The rapid growth of schools of business and their almost complete separation from the discipline of economics, out of which business administration emerged, may be instructive. Experience with the development of other emerging professions would seem to indicate that the separate school or program of public administration will likely be the most common format in the future.

Employment Characteristics and Public Service Education

From the 1940s through the 1970s, our economy moved relentlessly from the production of goods to the provision of services with an accompanying rapid growth in public service. This should not have been surprising given the general growth of the service side of the economy. All of the analyses of employment conditions in the United States during this period indicate that public employment was one of the top two or three major growth areas.

In the past ten years, there have been distinct shifts within these growth areas. For example, the civilian sector of the federal government has been stable at just under three million employees for the past five or six years. In addition, the federal civil service has been increasingly decentralized with fewer jobs in Washington and more jobs in the regional and area offices. There was a very dramatic spurt of growth in state government employment between the mid-1960s and the mid-1970s. That pattern of growth appears now to be slowing somewhat. As the growth in state employment begins to slow, there has been a speeding up of local government employment to include employment by counties and special jurisdictions. And, most important, we are now seeing the leveling off of public employment. Public education has begun to decline with the passage of the "baby boom" through the schools, and it will likely continue to decline given the sharp decline in population growth in the United States. And expenditure and revenue controls at the state level, such as Proposition 13 in California, have resulted in decline in state and local public employment.

It is important to remember that the public service is highly heterogeneous and relates directly to several different units in the university. Employees in the public works department come from schools of engineering, planners from schools or programs in planning, social workers from schools of social work, and so on. It is erroneous to assume that all of this growth is always connected with or is generally affected by public administration. But public administration employment has had growth along with the general growth in government. Public administration has tended to feed those parts of the public sector that have to do with the management functions—budgeting, purchasing, accounting, personnel administration, auditing, revenues, policy analysis, and the like. These have always been stable employment reservoirs for new M.P.A.s. Increasingly, however,

M.P.A.s are moving into what can be called "substantive administration" or "program administration." The M.P.A. who heads the social services department or the state environmental protection agency or the city police department is increasingly common. So it appears that the modern M.P.A. must know not only about management in the general sense, but probably would be advantaged by knowing how to manage some or another public service function.

Although public service employment is buoyant, and most new M.P.A.s find good jobs, there are problems.

Questions of Public Administration Pedagogy

There has been as much change in the character of education for public service as there has been growth in the field. These changes form an elaborate puzzle that can only be sketched here. Yet all these changes are more important to the quality of public service than are the preceding issues of the manner in which public programs are arranged in the university and the characteristics of the job market.

Probably the most basic and fundamental change in curriculum has to do with the professionalization and credentialing of public administrators. This follows quite naturally the other professions, particularly law, medicine, and education and even the newer professions, business administration, social work, and so forth, but there is a stark difference in the case of public administration, which is related to the origins of the field. Public administration grows out of political science, and political science is one of the social sciences and is a part of the liberal arts. It has long been held, tracing back to British higher education, that the best educational requisite for a first-quality public servant is a broad-gauged liberal arts education. During the early periods of the merit system in the United States, general managers were assumed to be an American version of a "gentleman administrator." With the development of the merit system in the United States, however, there has generally been a good mixture of liberal arts and substantive knowledge of organization theory, POSDCORB, and analytical skills.

Anyone reading the modern PACE (Professional and Administrative Career Examination) examination will be sensitive to the need for a well-developed knowledge of managerial or organizational theory and public service professionalism. This has had a profound impact on the nature of instruction, particularly for the M.P.A. degree. Initially, instruction was basically contextual in the form of developing in students a good knowledge of the workings of government. The M.P.A. degree that prepares generalists for public service is still relatively common, particularly in those programs given by political science departments. For decades, the staple pedagogical instrument was the case study, particularly case studies produced by the Inter-University Case Program.

The contextually generalized M.P.A. curriculum has been rapidly replaced by two other generalized curricula, both being cousins. The first is the M.P.A. program that prepares the management generalist, the second is the program that prepares the policy analyst. The management generalist gets a heavy dose of organization theory, leadership, interpersonal skills, budgeting, personnel, computer utilization, analytic techniques, and economics. The M.P.A. program with a policy analysis generalization runs a bit lighter on the management subjects and heavier on quantitative skills, economics, and computer technology. Several of the newer schools of public administration, particularly Minnesota, Michigan, Berkeley, Carnegie-Mellon, and Texas, are strongly inclined toward the policy analysis generalization.

One of the more interesting aspects of the lexicon of these schools is that they use the phrase "public administration" as seldom as possible. In the university pecking order, policy analysis, the management of public policy, and policy skills are regarded as a higher status form of instruction. Public administration is, in the minds of many, still connected with a "nuts and bolts" approach to the routine of day-to-day government management. Thus, though there is clearly a movement away from the generalist administrator and the contextual curriculum, the management and policy analysis generalizations that are now in vogue still seem to impress upon the student and upon the potential employer (and most likely on their university colleagues) the significance of public affairs education. After all, public administration is not vocational.

A recent essay by John Brandl, an economist who is just now stepping down after several years as the first director of the School of Public Affairs of the University of Minnesota, is instructive:

> Then, in the brief period, 1968–71, at each of a dozen or so major universities it was decided to revamp or replace a public administration program by founding a new institute or school of public affairs or public policy. Why at this time? To an unprecedented degree the formulation and evaluation of federal domestic policy in the 1960's had involved applied social science. The Great Society, a marriage of the New Deal and Social Engineering, had followed, and to some degree mimicked the introduction of cost effectiveness analysis, planning, programming and budgeting systems, and sophisticated computer techniques in our Department of Defense under Secretary Robert MacNamara. A new school teaching these approaches could be sophisticated, eclectic, useful, quantitative—respectable.[3]

Such "respectable" programs have grown and developed and are now flourishing, and they will no doubt continue to do so. It is a best guess, however, that they will be but one approach to public administration. Probably the dominant approach will continue to be the combination of the science of government with the science of management (this separates the subject of management from the subject of analysis). And a corollary to this will be a "policy specialization" or some level of substantive expertise for the M.P.A. student, such as in the fields of urban administration, environmental administration, public safety, and so on. There will doubtless continue to be the argument that public administration is neither a field, profession, nor discipline.[4] I am of the view that public administration is certainly not a discipline, nor should it be. If it is not a profession, it certainly has taken on many of the characteristics of a profession, and if it is not an interdisciplinary field, then there probably is no such thing. But it is clear that there is no body of theory that presently dominates the subject. Thus it is possible to argue that there is an intellectual crisis in public administration.[5] There is probably only an intellectual crisis if one assumes that there must be a single, agreed-upon paradigm to which all in the field are committed. For example, the discipline of economics has had a very heavy influence in schools of public policy or policy analysis. Again, it is interesting to quote John Brandl as he retires from directing a policy and quantitatively oriented school of public affairs:

> There is something disciplinarily imperialistic about economics in a school of public policy. Its formal elegance and practical usefulness give it a central role, if only for pedagogical purposes. Its shortcomings, though great, do not create a search for a new discipline. There can be no discipline of public policy analysis precisely because at the heart of its subject are the alternative points of view with which people perceive and deal with public affairs. A school of public policy ought to be preparing its students for entry into a profession, not a discipline. The challenge is not to develop single general frameworks for confronting issues, but to enable students to develop their own convictions while coming to understand a variety of ways of perceiving and dealing with public affairs.[6]

It is a best guess, then, that public administration education over the near-term future will involve a dialogue between several models or paradigms. Certainly the human resources approach to public administration is well developed and has many significant theorists and adherents. The politics of administration approach is similarly well developed, particularly by those political scientists with a strong interest in policy and administration. The public choice economists have a strong conviction of their views. It is probable that the field will experience a period of strong interaction between and among these points of view. Thus, rather than being an empirically or theoretically barren field, public administration is in fact the reverse. Public administration is rich with theories and perspectives, and, like the fields of medicine and education, there is probably no need for these to be one single agreed-upon theory. The point is that those who manage the affairs of government are engaged in highly varied and differing activities. No single theory or concept could possibly hope to comprehend all of these activities.

Most programs in public administration provide for specializations, concentrations, or minors. Several of these specializations have to do with the management functions— budgeting, personnel, and so forth. Others have to do with policy fields such as law enforcement, international affairs, environmental affairs, urban affairs, health administration, and the like. Indeed, certain schools have taken the name of their specializations, such as the Graduate School of International and Public Affairs, the School of Public and Environmental Affairs, the School of Urban Affairs. These specializations customarily constitute as much as fifteen hours of course work and frequently attract the attention of potential employers, at least in terms of a presumption that the products of these programs are able to do some specific thing straightaway and are not generalists. The old public administration phrase "a specialist in generalization" has long since disappeared from the lexicon and the curriculum. In *The Future Executive*, Harlan Cleveland tried to resurrect it by pressing for the public administration person who "sees the situation as a whole."[7]

A long-standing issue in education for the public service has to do with the level of government being targeted by the curriculum in question. For example, the University of Kansas and the University of Southern California programs in public administration have presumed to prepare people for local government management, and particularly for city management. The Kennedy, Wilson, and Maxwell Schools have had a heavy emphasis, until recent years, on federal employment. To some extent, their curricula reflect these levels of employment, but the emphasis is relatively light. Probably the most overworked generalization in curriculum terms is city management. There are fewer than twenty-five hundred city managers in the United States, so to use city managers as the prototype public administrator is both misleading and pedagogically weak. If anything, city management is a highly unique public service responsibility. Most other public service responsibilities are vastly more typical, at least in terms of organization theory. One is left to wonder why we continue a fascination in public administration curricula with the city manager.

The second problem is not unlike the first. The very heavy emphasis in public administration literature and in the classroom on federal decision making and the national government responsibilities is pronounced. What is seldom made clear is the fact that the federal government is rarely at the delivery level of a given public service. General and grand policy may be made by the national government and possibly carried out at the state and local levels. It is illogical to assume that a student's knowledge of, say, national health policy will be of any particular use should the student end up managing a neighborhood health center. In sum, public administration is still very much in the process of sorting out the level of government issue as it relates to curriculum.

Of all of the graduate fields of American higher education, certainly public administration has been one of the most inventive and aggressive. The development of mid-career or in-career programs in the field at the graduate level in public administration in most of the major cities of the United States has made an enormous difference not only on education for the public service, but on the practice of public administration. In this way, many bridges are built from the public service professions to public administration. In 1973 in-career students were almost exactly half of those studying public administration; in 1976 there were more in-career than pre-career students. The practicing public official with a baccalaureate in engineering can choose to take a master's in public administration not only because of a recognition that he or she is engaged in public administration, but also because the master's degree in public administration is available in a mid-career and innovative way, whereas the master's in engineering or in public works probably is not. The long-term impact of our innovative mid-career programs in public administration education will probably have more fully affected the development of a broad concept of the field than any other single factor. The phrase "public administration is everyone's second profession" is already trite. Many persons who originally identified with one or another of the public service professions now have moved up the hierarchy and are clearly practicing public administration, identifying primarily with public administration and secondarily with their original policy or nonmanagement specialization.

These are just a few of the curriculum issues facing public administration. Fortunately, the field is buoyant, and the prospects for improving are great. The National Association of Schools of Public Affairs and Administration, representing the schools in the field, has now adopted guidelines and standards for the master's degree in public administration. These guidelines and standards will at a minimum serve as a common referent by which schools can engage in self-evaluation, can go through the process of articulating the premises behind their curricula, and can set their sights on improvement. Furthermore, these guidelines call for the publishing of the characteristics of different programs and will enable schools to learn from one another. If public administration is increasingly to professionalize, the work of NASPAA will have contributed significantly to that goal.

Relations Among Education for Public Administration, the Rest of Higher Education, and the Public Service

As public administration increasingly professionalizes, it will likely take on the characteristics associated with other professional schools and programs. It should be logical to expect the development of boards of visitors to advise deans and faculty on the content of curriculum. It should be logical to expect efforts to carve out special places or special status in the public service for the recipients of public administration degrees. It should not surprise the reader to know that many public service responsibilities require a specific degree before one can take a given position, as is the case in certain social work responsibilities, in teaching, in law, and so on. It is logical to expect that schools and programs in public administration will press for job descriptions that include a requirement for the holding of a degree.

If there is a lack in contemporary public administration education it is the weakness of its empirical base. Because the field primarily borrows from the disciplines and from other professions, most of the empirical work on which public administration draws is done within the disciplines. Consequently, many important subjects "fall between the slats." For example, we do not have a rich body of knowledge about the interaction between line and staff agencies in a public bureaucracy. On the other hand, we know in great detail about the determinants of expenditures for education or the relationship between worker morale and productivity. As public administration education develops, it will likely grow empirically and begin to fill in the spaces between the slats. A simple review of these points is set out in Table 7.

Conclusions

Is it assumed that the improvement of the public service will result in a general increase in the capacity or effectiveness of governments? All of the trends, activities, and strategies discussed above must be judged in the light of this objective. It should not be assumed that there is a causal relationship between the growth and development of education for public administration and the quality of government. It is at this level that there must be a dialectic. To use another profession as an analogue, can we assume that the

Table 7. Education in the New Public Administration

From	Transition	To
M.P.A. programs closely connected to political science	Separate public administration programs	Public administration programs bridged to or connected with other public service educational programs such as social work, public health, planning, etc.
Pre-career education for public administration	Mid-career education for public administration	Continued education for public management
Public administration education for management or staff functions	Public administration education as the development of analytic skills	Public administration linking management and substantive specialization such as urban, international, environmental, etc.
Public administration education as POSD-CORB and "the principles"	Public administration education highly situational, as human relations, as policy analysis, as management science, etc. The groping for a model.	Public administration as a paradigmatic dialogue
Emphasis on administration in public administration education	Emphasis on neutral analysis and description in public administration education	Emphasis on ethics and the public interest in public administration education

general health of the populace has been improved by the presence and growth of schools of medicine? Can the same be said in the fields of law and education? This is, after all, an arguable question. It is further an arguable point whether the quality of government has an enhancing effect on the quality of life. It seems incumbent upon the professional public administration educator to be able to posit, articulate, and defend the assertion of a positive correlation between education for public administration and the quality of government and to demonstrate with clarity these relationships. Without such a dialectic, education for the public service will become hollow and self-serving.

New public administration and the values associated with social equity hold, I believe, the greatest potential for improving government practices and hence the quality of life. It is through the universities, and particularly through the modern programs in public administration, that these concepts and values are being taught.

7: Public Administration in the 1980s

Perhaps the most widespread
limitation on the administrative
process results when participants
define administration as *office-holding* rather than an essential
ingredient in organizational
accomplishment.—James D. Thompson,
Organizations in Action

This consideration of new public administration will conclude with a consideration of two very general questions.
First, what will public administration be like in the coming
decade and in the coming generation? Second, what should
public administration be like in the coming decade and in the
coming generation? Although stated separately, these questions not only overlap but completely blend to become the
same question: What kind of a public administration will we
create for ourselves in the coming decade and in the coming
generation?

William G. Scott and David K. Hart in their remarkably
perceptive study, *Organizational America,* point out that the
twentieth century has been the American century. Our
dominance in this century has resulted from high technology
and the perfection of organizational skills.[1] Our increasingly
large and complex nation seems to have called forth large
and complex organizations to make it work. Our lives are
surrounded by those massive human-technical engines we
call organizations. How can we make those engines (our
engines) respond to the issues and problems of the 1980s?

If we are to meet these issues, we must recognize that
organizations function fundamentally in the realm of values.
The traditional values of public administration have served

us well, standing the test of time. The value of efficiency—as much utility as can be gotten for a given level of resources—will always be a part of the foundations of public administration. So, too, will the value of economy—expending as few resources as possible for a given or desired level of productivity—endure. We will continue to emphasize the values associated with effective and rational decision-making processes, whereby our organizations can be made productive. And we shall continue to value the normative context in which the public organizations function: first, the ultimate responsibility of elected officials for making public choices; second, the constitutional authority of the courts to be the ultimate interpreters of the law; third, the legitimacy of all those groups whose interests are negotiated through public policy-making processes; fourth, the rights and dignity of each individual citizen; fifth, a commitment to an economic system that provides for full employment at fair wages and that supports the provision of housing, consumer goods, and economic growth which fosters general prosperity and well-being. These traditional values will be as important in the 1980s as they have been in the past. But, although they are necessary, they are not sufficient.

To be effective in the 1980s, public organizations will need to be significantly more responsive. The key to responsiveness is organizational adaptability to change. The processes of social, economic, and political change will continue to accelerate, making it vitally important that organizations adapt. One of the key criteria for effective leadership in the modern organization will be facilitating the processes of organizational adaption. Top-quality leaders must learn to anticipate social, economic, and political change and to capitalize on it. There will be conditions under which the patterns of change will require organizational growth. But there will be equally as many and perhaps more situations in which these change processes will require organizational decline, cutback, and devolution. The good manager in the 1980s will be effective at scanning the political, economic, and social horizons and leading the processes of adaption to growth or decline. To do this, leaders will need to know modern technology and particularly the technologies of communication. But if they are to be effective, they cannot become the captives of computers, telephones, and television. Organizational change is more likely to be the result of imaginative policies and difficult economic, political, and social choices than the application of technological solutions.

The effective public administrator will continue to be the "rational calculator" of alternative ways to achieve public objectives. But there will be increasing recognition of the competing and conflictual nature of public objectives, of the tension between majority rule and minority rights, and of the apparent continual need to provide more public services with fewer resources. Administrative rationality will come increasingly to mean agreement as to specific public programs and the volume of services rather than abstract notions of goals and objectives. This will require the administrator to be fully involved in the processes of choice making and planning. Good administrators will be planners, and the processes of planning and administration will blend. The administrator will know that it is possible to do many things with the organization. But, this alone is not sufficient rationale for trying to do everything. The key will be knowing what to do and how much of it to do.

To some, this portrait of the modern public administrator is alarming. Indeed, Victor Thompson has suggested that those associated with new public administration are engaged in a "brazen attempt to 'steal' the popular sovereignty."[2] He imagines a political, economic, and social world in which public administrators operate as value-free functionaries in carrying out executive and legislative mandates. Nonsense. Public administrators are not, nor should they be, "neutral" robots carrying out a public policy they have no part in making. Their jobs are not like the jobs of umpires or referees. They are, in fact, players. They are the experts hired to carry out the public will. Can you ask a skilled and highly trained person such as a school superintendent to be neutral about education? I certainly would not want such a superintendent nor, I imagine, would anyone else. If the superintendent is not neutral, then what ought to be his or her values? We would assume a strong and continuing dedication to education. We would assume a dedication and commitment to efficiency, economy, and rationality; and we would likewise assume a commitment to the provision of educational services on an equitable basis. You would expect the superintendent, as the resident local expert on educational matters, to be fully involved in the making of educational policy, involved with the citizens through their sundry interest groups, involved with the school board and other elected officials, involved with state and federal agencies whose responsibilities are relevant to education. If we ask the superintendent to be skilled and effective in the provision of education, then can we ask that he or she have no interest whatever in the issue of education for whom? New public administration holds to the view that the superintendent should be at the center of this issue, deeply concerned with the distributive question and with the social, economic, and political ramifications of that question. The superintendent should provide leadership and advocate both good education and good education for all.

Although this perspective is associated in this book with the so-called new public administration, it is my view that the finest public servants have always functioned in the manner just described. Rather than stealing the public sovereignty, they are enabling the fullest expression of that sovereignty for the widest range of citizens.

The Individual and the Organization

Two recent and significant studies of contemporary organizations in America come to essentially similar conclusions. Our world is increasingly dominated by organizations. We are experiencing what Scott and Hart call the organizational imperative. They note:

No contemporary issue is more important than the problems of values that have emerged with the growing dominance of modern organizations: the substitution of the values of the organization for the values of the individual, and the concomitant emergence of a new and indispensable power elite of managers. None of this should surprise us, for we have had ample warning. The impact of modern organization on American values began to receive considerable attention in the 1950s, a decade much condemned for complacency and Babbittry. . . . In the early 1970s it again began to dawn upon some that an apparent implacable force had been set in motion: the modern organization, a reality more powerful than religion, politics, and economics, in which managers perform a uniquely modern role. They are the human intermediaries between the modern organization and the mass of producing-consuming citizens. Managers must reconcile the needs of the organization through the efficient use of resources to increase material goods and services. The successful performance of this function has been the primary basis for the legitimacy of modern organizations, public and private. Through it, managers have assumed a new role as the mediators of legitimacy.

By now, however, modern organizations move with an inertial dialectic all their own, and the individuals trapped by such mammoth governments—or corporations or universities—are apparently powerless either to affect them or to escape from them. To survive in this new order of things, all must conform to the requirements of the modern organizations, and therein lies the problem.[3]

A big issue, then, is the dignity, worth, and importance of both the individual working within the organization and the individual whose needs are presumably served by that organization.

After a brilliant analysis of our organizational condition, Scott and Hart conclude with what they call The Probable Future, the primary feature of which is the Drift into Totalitarian America. They argue that "the modern organization is the essential feature of totalitarianism because it is the primary means of control."[4] They further argue that the only reason we are not now in a fully organized state and the totalitarian takeover has not yet been completed is that there is a "residue of commitment to the individual values of our past that has prevented the complete domination by modern organization. This compulsion to eradicate what remains of individualism in values is bringing America to the edge of a modern revolution."[5]

They then ask the question, "Who will challenge the organizational imperative?" Scott and Hart conclude that reform will not come from the significant people primarily because it is not in their interest to be the authors of reform. They also dismiss the insignificant people because they lack power, because they are the primary beneficiaries of employment in modern organization, and because they are "constantly told of their good fortune at being able to consume an unending flow of consumer products."[6] Scott and Hart finally conclude the "practicality of reform by the *professional people*":

Reform can come from the professionals because mass support for change is growing and they have the technical and organizational expertise to galvanize this support into a reform movement. They are in the right place at the right time with the right skills, yet will the professionals accept the responsibility that has been thrust upon them? There is a chance to avoid the trap of totalitarian America. The professionals are correctly positioned to be the dynamic force behind social change. If they do not rise to this responsibility, reform will never come. They could lead this revolution because many of them are still young enough to be receptive to new ideas, they have a common managerial language and technique, they understand organizations and how to "organize and coordinate masses of people for effective action" and, most important, the professionals are close enough to the insignificant people, both on and off the job, that they can empathize with their difficulties and their aspirations. Using the time-worn model of an oppressed working class, the radicals of the 1960s could not forge an effective coalition with the insignificant people. They could not understand them as the professionals can.[7]

To accomplish this, the professionals must first recognize that they will never be significant people, but will likely always be relatively stable specialists. They will need to understand that they will be followers. They will need to work together voluntarily and in some cases "collectively challenge the conservatism of the significant people."[8] Finally, the professionals' "new attitudes about their life's work require a foundation of values and a changed perception of the innateness of human nature. This means that in some respects the professionals must become philosophers, and this is a role for which they have not been trained. Yet the philosophical task must precede action; and if philosophers will not become managers, it is certain that managers must become philosophers."[9] Finally, Scott and Hart conclude that the place for the preparation of the modern administration is in the schools of management and administration.

Scott and Hart's conclusions closely parallel the point of view presented in Chapter 6 of this book. It is in the schools of management and administration where concepts of the sharing of authority, the job as a satisfactory individual experience, and the collective design and operation of work environments are taught. Similarly, it is in the schools where basic concepts of citizens' rights, citizen involvement in organizational decision making, and other notions of the individual as citizen are developed. And it is in the schools where professionals learn the skills of scanning organizational boundaries and gauging the political, economic, and social horizons so as to work collectively to keep the organization changeful and responsive. No amount of high-quality internal management can compensate for a failure correctly to gauge the processes of change at the organization's boundaries and enable the organization to respond.

The modern professional will also need to learn the geography of public administration. The key to citizen involvement is to develop, nurture, and protect patterns of decentralization, forcing decision making as close as possible to the individual citizen. The professional will need to understand public service not so much as the care, feeding, development, and growth of an organization but rather the management of a project or a cluster of projects designed to carry out specific activities designed to meet individual citizens' needs—needs that will likely be in the process of change.

Victor Thompson's recent analysis of organizations focuses heavily on their roles and functions. He observes correctly that large-scale organizations can have a dehumanizing effect on individuals working for them and served by them.[10] The problem in Thompson's view is the failure of the organization to respond in a compassionate way to individuals. He cites countless examples of the mindless application of organizational rules to the unnecessary detriment of workers and citizens. He is generally pessimistic about a wide range of possible "solutions" to the problem of individual compassion in a world of mass organization. He dismisses management training, as well as the techniques of personnel administration. He holds out some small hope for organizational development and sensitivity training. He generally is negative toward the potential for smaller units of government, smaller agencies and organizations, and decentralized organizations to be more compassionate. He finds little potential in combining the roles of manager, worker, and citizen in a single individual. Thompson is no less skeptical about the potentials of the ombudsman to deal fundamentally with the problem of compassion. And, finally, he is most particularly critical of the activist and involved approach of the so-called new public administration.

Although Thompson paints a particularly pessimistic picture, his last chapter begins this way: "This account will by now have impressed the reader as hopelessly pessimistic. Actually, the reality of the situation is not so bad as it appears. The fact is, most people do not suffer unduly at the hands of large, modern bureaucratic organizations."[11] Thompson holds out some hope for a natural combination of the individual with the organization: "As individuals change in our changing culture and feel less strongly the need for an organization to be like a family, more and more people will work in more and more organizations that are in some ways more like families. Man and his institutions will fit one another better. A perfect fit we can never expect short of genetic or behavioral engineering. Such engineering is a long way off. We have not yet decided how to select either the engineers or the design."[12]

Thompson has gone too far in anthropomorphizing the organization. He has it so completely independent of the people of whom it is composed that it somehow comes to exist external from them and independent of them. He is wrong. If individuals have the wits to create these structures and all the technologies that accompany them, they surely have the wits to make them responsive, adaptable, effective, and humane. But we should have no illusions. Controlling these giant, human, technical engines to get them to do what we want is difficult, and it will become more difficult.

No doubt one of the biggest issues of the 1980s will be productivity. All present indications are that the ratio of goods and services produced to manpower expended is declining. More and more people in the workforce are producing less and less. A corollary issue will compound this problem. We are in the era of limits, no growth, and see around us a pervasive attitude toward cutting back on expenditures and presumably on government services. It will be exceedingly difficult to deal with the needs of the individual worker, most particularly in the public service, if more and more is expected for less and less. Individual citizens cannot expect to have their services increased, while depriving public employees of their well-being. On the one hand, public employees cannot assume that government organizations exist for their own care and feeding. Indeed, public administration exists to provide public services. But the citizens cannot expect a dedicated public service without having to pay for it.

The problem of productivity, coupled with the problem of revenue and expenditure cutbacks, could lessen the potentials for social equity. If there is less and less generally, there will be less and less to go around. If history is any guide, under conditions of cutback or austerity, those at the lower end of the social and economic spectrum receive the least. We are entering an era in which it is critically important that public officials be cognizant of the rights of individual citizens to receive an equitable share of public services.

Notes

Foreword

1. James C. Charlesworth, ed., *The Theory and Practice of Public Administration: Scope, Objectives, and Methods* (Philadelphia: The American Academy of Political and Social Science, October 1968), p. ix.

2. Ibid., pp. 3–7.

3. Dwight Waldo, "Developments in Public Administration," *Annals of the American Academy of Political and Social Science*, 404 (November 1972), 238.

Chapter 1

1. Woodrow Wilson, "The Study of Administration," *Political Science Quarterly*, 2, no. 1 (June 1887) as reprinted in 56 (December 1941), 493–509.

2. Leonard D. White, *Introduction to the Study of Public Administration* (New York: Macmillan Company, 1926).

3. John C. Honey, "A Report: Higher Education for Public Service," *Public Administration Review*, 27 (November 1967), 294–321; Frederick C. Mosher, *Democracy and the Public Service* (New York: Oxford University Press, 1968).

4. Herbert Kaufman, "Administrative Decentralization and Political Power," *Public Administration Review*, 29 (January–February 1969), 3–15.

5. Dwight Waldo, "Scope of the Theory of Public Administration," in James C. Charlesworth, ed., *Theory and Practice of Public Administration: Scope, Objectives and Methods* (Philadelphia: The American Academy of Political and Social Science, October 1968), pp. 1–26.

6. Ibid.

7. Anthony Downs, *Inside Bureaucracy* (Boston: Little, Brown, 1967).

8. See especially Charles L. Schultze, *The Politics and Economics of Public Spending* (Washington, D.C.: The Brookings Institution, 1969), and Aaron Wildavsky, *The Politics of the Budgetary Process* (Boston: Little, Brown, 1974).

Ke 69. A3

1980-13-82-83

cl. 167

9. Charles Lindbloom, *The Intelligence of Democracy* (New York: The Free Press, 1966).

10. See especially James March and Herbert Simon, *Organizations* (New York: John Wiley & Sons, 1958).

Chapter 2

1. Frank Marini, ed., *Toward a New Public Administration* (San Francisco: Chandler Publishing Co., 1971); Dwight Waldo, *Public Administration in a Time of Turbulence* (San Francisco: Chandler Publishing Co., 1971); H. George Frederickson, *Neighborhood Control in the 1970s* (New York: Chandler Publishing Co., 1973).

2. An interesting example is the compilation of an excellent bibliography in public administration. The bibliography items selected for annotation were based on a sample survey of books used by teachers of public administration. Less than half the books could be categorized as political science. See Howard E. McCurdy, *Public Administration: A Bibliography* (Washington, D.C.: The College of Public Affairs, The American University, 1972).

3. See especially Dwight Waldo, "Developments in Public Administration," *Annals of the American Academy of Political and Social Science*, 404 (November 1972), 217–245.

4. Frances E. Rourke, *Bureaucracy, Politics and Public Policy*, 2d ed. (Boston: Little, Brown, 1976), pp. 183–184.

5. Thomas Kuhn, *The Structure of Scientific Revolutions* (Chicago: University of Chicago Press, 1970).

6. See the "Symposium on Productivity in Government," *Public Administration Review*, 32, no. 6 (November–December 1972), 739–851.

7. Frederick C. Mosher, *Governmental Reorganizations: Cases and Commentary* (Indianapolis: Bobbs-Merrill, 1967).

8. Herbert Wilcox, "The Cultural Traits of Hierarchy in Middle Class Children," *Public Administration Review*, 29, no. 2 (March–April 1968), 222–235.

9. See Herbert Simon, *Administrative Behavior* (New York: Macmillan Company, 1957), and *Models of Man* (New York: John Wiley & Sons, 1956); James March and Herbert Simon, *Organizations* (New York: John Wiley & Sons, 1958); Richard Cyert and

James March, *A Behavioral Theory of the Firm* (Englewood Cliffs, N.J.: Prentice-Hall, 1963).

10. See "Symposium on Productivity in Government," pp. 739–851.

11. This designation is taken from Charles Perrow, *Complex Organizations: A Critical Essay* (Glenview, Ill.: Scott, Foresman, 1972).

12. James Thompson, *Organizations in Action: The Social Science Bases of Administrative Theory* (New York: McGraw-Hill, 1967).

13. Frederick C. Mosher, *Democracy and the Public Service* (New York: Oxford University Press, 1968).

14. Amitai Etzioni, *A Comparative Analysis of Complex Organizations* (New York: The Free Press, 1961).

15. Charles Lindbloom, *The Intelligence of Democracy: Decision-Making Through Mutual Adjustment* (New York: The Free Press, 1965).

16. Rensis Likert, *The Human Organization: Its Management and Value* (New York: McGraw-Hill, 1967); Daniel Katz and Robert Kahn, *The Social Psychology of Organizations* (New York: John Wiley & Sons, 1966).

17. David K. Hart and William G. Scott, "The Moral Nature of Man in Organizations: A Comparative Analysis," *The Academy of Management Journal*, 14, no. 2 (June 1971), 241–255.

18. Vincent Ostrom, *The Intellectual Crisis in American Public Administration* (University, Ala.: University of Alabama Press, 1973).

19. Ibid., pp. 28–29.

20. Ibid., pp. 111–112.

Chapter 3

1. There is a kind of "holy grail" quality to some of this work, as in seeking the new public administration in existential thought, or in phenomenology. Although these philosophies surely bear on contemporary public administration, they are hardly the holy grail.

2. See especially the works of Robert Bish, Vincent and Elinor Ostrom, and Roger Albrandt.

3. See H. George Frederickson, ed., "Curriculum Essays on Citizens, Politics and Administration in Urban Neighborhoods,"

Public Administration Review, Special Issue, 32 (November 1972).

4. Dwight Waldo, "Developments in Public Administration," *Annals of the American Academy of Political and Social Science*, 404 (November 1972), 224.

5. Henry Campbell Black, *Black's Law Dictionary*, 4th ed. (St. Paul, Minn.: West, 1957), p. 634.

6. John Rawls, *A Theory of Justice* (Cambridge, Mass: The Belknap Press of Harvard University Press, 1971), p. 7.

7. Ibid., pp. 3–4.

8. Ibid., p. 176.

9. Ibid., p. 137.

10. David K. Hart, "Social Equity, Justice and the Equitable Administrator," *Public Administration Review*, 34 (January–February 1974), 6.

11. Rawls, *Theory of Justice*, p. 135.

12. Hart, "Social Equity," p. 7.

13. Rawls, *Theory of Justice*, p. 76.

14. Hart, "Social Equity," p. 8.

15. Rawls, *Theory of Justice*, p. 102.

16. Hart, "Social Equity," p. 8.

17. Ibid., pp. 9–10.

18. *Griggs* v. *Duke Power Co.*, 401 U.S., 424, 433 (March 8, 1971).

19. Ibid.

20. Eugene B. McGregor, "Social Equity and the Public Service," *Public Administration Review*, 34 (January–February 1974), 23–24.

21. *Hawkins* v. *Town of Shaw*, 427 F.2d 1286 (5th Cir. 1971) aff'd 461 F.2d 1171 (1972) (en banc).

22. *Serrano* v. *Priest*, 487 P2d 1241 (1972).

23. *Rodriguez* v. *San Antonio*, U.S. Supreme Court, March 21, 1972. On this subject see especially David O. Porter and Teddy Wood Porter, "Social Equity and Fiscal Federalism," *Public Administration Review*, 34 (January–February 1974), 36–43.

24. Stephen R. Chitwood, "Social Equity and Social Service Productivity," *Public Administration Review*, 34 (January–February 1974), 29–35.

25. Richard Chapman and Frederic N. Cleaveland, *Meeting the Needs of Tomorrow's Public Service: Guidelines for Professional Education in Public Administration* (Washington, D.C.: National Academy of Public Administration, January 1973).

26. Vincent Ostrom, *The Intellectual Crisis in American Public Administration* (University, Ala.: University of Alabama Press, 1973).

Chapter 4

1. Victor A. Thompson, *Modern Organization* (New York: Alfred A. Knopf, 1961); James D. Thompson, *Organizations in Action: The Social Science Bases of Administrative Theory* (New York: McGraw-Hill, 1967); Anthony Downs, *Inside Bureaucracy* (Boston: Little, Brown, 1967).
2. (Indianapolis: Bobbs-Merrill, 1967).
3. Christopher Jencks et al., *Inequality: A Reassessment of the Effect of Family and Schooling in America* (New York: Basic Books, 1972).
4. The use of tables of this sort appears to have originated with Emory Olson. It was adapted and used much as appears here by John Pfiffner and Frank Sherwood, *Administrative Organization* (Englewood Cliffs, N.J.: Prentice-Hall, 1960), p. 108. Some of the items used in this essay are adapted from the Pfiffner-Sherwood book. A later application of this procedure was developed by Robert J. Biller, "Converting Knowledge into Action: Toward a Postindustrial Society," in Jong S. Jun and William B. Storm, eds., *Tomorrow's Organizations: Challenges and Strategies* (Glenview, Ill.: Scott, Foresman, 1973). Many of the statements found in the tables presented above are from the Biller essay, with some modifications.
5. *Administrative Behavior* (New York: Macmillan Co., 1957).
6. *The Intelligence of Democracy: Decision Making through Mutual Adjustment* (New York: The Free Press, 1965).
7. "Mixed Scanning: A 'Third' Approach to Decision-Making," *Public Administration Review*, 27, no. 5 (December 1967), 386–387.
8. Harlan Cleveland, *The Future Executive: A Guide for Tomorrow's Managers* (New York: Harper & Row, 1972), p. 88.

Chapter 5

1. Max Weber, *The Theory of Social and Economic Organization*, translated by A. M. Henderson and Talcott Parsons (Fair Lawn, N.J.: Oxford University Press, 1947).

2. F. J. Roethlisberger and W. J. Dickson, *Management and the Worker* (Cambridge, Mass.: Harvard University Press, 1939).

3. William H. Reed, "The Decline of the Hierarchy in Industrial Organizations," in David I. Clelland and William R. King, *Systems, Organizations, Analysis, Management* (New York: McGraw-Hill, 1969), p. 22; Warren G. Bennis, "The Coming Death of Bureaucracy," in ibid., p. 12; Warren G. Bennis, "Post-Bureaucratic Leadership," *Trans-Action*, July–August 1969, p. 44.

4. Rensis Likert, *Human Organization: Its Management and Value* (New York: McGraw-Hill, 1967).

5. T. George Harris, "Organic Populism: A Conversation with Warren G. Bennis," *Psychology Today*, February 1970, p. 48.

6. Peter Drucker, *The Age of Discontinuity: Guidelines to a Changing Society* (New York: Harper & Row, 1969); Warren G. Bennis and Philip E. Slater, *The Temporary Society* (New York: Harper & Row, 1968).

7. Robert L. Lineberry and Edmund P. Fowler, "Reformism and Public Policies in American Cities," *American Political Science Review*, 67 (September 1967), 702.

8. G. Robert Crain, Elihu Katz, and D. B. Rosenthal, *The Politics of Community Conflict* (Indianapolis: Bobbs-Merrill, 1969).

9. Herbert Kaufman, "Administrative Decentralization and Political Power," *Public Administration Review*, 29 (January–February 1969), 3–15.

10. John Pfiffner and Frank Sherwood, *Administrative Organization* (Englewood Cliffs, N.J.: Prentice-Hall, 1960), pp. 189–205.

11. Dwight Ink, "A Management Crisis for the New President: People Programs," *Public Administration Review*, 28, no. 6 (November–December 1968), 546–552.

12. James Fesler, *Area and Administration* (University, Ala.: University of Alabama Press, 1949), pp. 8–18.

13. Charles M. Hardin, *Food and Fiber in American Politics* (Washington, D.C.: U.S. Government Printing Office, 1968); James Davis and Kenneth Dolbeare, *Little Groups of Neighbors: The Selective Service System* (Chicago: Markham Press, 1968).

14. William H. Riker, *Federalism: Origin, Operation, Significance* (Boston: Little, Brown, 1964).

15. Larry Kirkhart, "Public Administration and Selected Developments in Social Science: Toward a Theory of Public Adminis-

tration," in Frank Marini, ed., *Toward a New Public Administration: The Minnowbrook Perspective* (San Francisco: Chandler Publishing Co., 1971), pp. 127–163.

16. Harris, "Organic Populism."

17. Rensis Likert, *New Patterns of Management* (New York: McGraw-Hill, 1961), p. 105.

18. Likert, *The Human Organization*, pp. 160–166.

19. For a full treatment of the suburbs as a model for neighborhood control see David Perry, "The Suburb as a Model for Neighborhood Control," in George Frederickson, *Neighborhood Control in the 1970s* (New York: Chandler Publishing Co., 1973), pp. 85–100.

20. Frederickson, *Neighborhood Control*; Milton Kotler, *Neighborhood Government: The Local Foundations of Political Life* (Indianapolis and New York: Bobbs-Merrill, 1969); Charles S. Benson and Peter B. Lund, *Neighborhood Distribution of Local Public Services* (Berkeley, Calif.: Institute of Government Studies, University of California, Berkeley, 1969).

21. David I. Clelland and William R. King, *Systems Analysis and Project Management* (New York: McGraw-Hill, 1968); David I. Clelland and William R. King, *Systems, Organizations, Analysis, Management: A Book of Readings* (New York: McGraw-Hill, 1969); George A. Steiner and William G. Ryan, *Industrial Project Management* (New York: Macmillan Co., 1968); John Stanley Baumgartner, *Project Management* (Homewood, Ill.: Irwin, 1963).

22. Committee for Economic Development, *Reshaping Government in Metropolitan Areas* (New York: Committee for Economic Development, 1970).

23. Vincent Ostrom, Charles Tiebout, and Robert Warren, "The Organization of Government in Metropolitan Areas: A Theoretical Inquiry," *American Political Science Review* 61 (December 1961), 831–842. See also Anthony Downs, *An Economic Theory of Democracy* (New York: Harper & Row, 1957), and James W. Buchanan and Gordon Tullock, *The Calculus of Consent* (Ann Arbor: University of Michigan Press, 1962).

Chapter 6

1. Richard Chapman and Frederic N. Cleaveland, *Meeting the Needs of Tomorrow's Public Service: Guidelines for Professional*

Education in Public Administration (Washington, D.C.: National Academy of Public Administration, 1973).

2. Alice Stone and Donald Stone, "Appendix: Case Histories of Early Professional Education Programs," in Frederick C. Mosher, ed., *American Public Administration: Past, Present, Future* (University, Ala.: University of Alabama Press, 1975), pp. 268–289.

3. "Public Service Education in the 1970's," School of Public Affairs, University of Minnesota, Mimeo, January 1976, p. 2.

4. Richard L. Schott, "Public Administration as a Profession: Problems and Prospects," *Public Administration Review*, 36, no. 3 (May–June 1976), 253–259.

5. Vincent Ostrom, *The Intellectual Crisis in American Public Administration* (University, Ala.: University of Alabama Press, 1973).

6. Brandl, "Public Service Education," pp. 7–8.

7. Harlan Cleveland, *The Future Executive: A Guide for Tomorrow's Managers* (New York: Harper & Row, 1972).

Chapter 7

1. William G. Scott and David K. Hart, *Organizational America* (Boston: Houghton Mifflin Co., 1979).

2. Victor A. Thompson, *Without Sympathy or Enthusiasm* (University, Ala.: University of Alabama Press, 1975), p. 66.

3. Scott and Hart, *Organizational America*, pp. 6–7.

4. Ibid., p. 211.

5. Ibid., p. 209.

6. Ibid., p. 219.

7. Ibid., pp. 220–221.

8. Ibid., pp. 223–224.

9. Ibid., p. 225.

10. Thompson, *Without Sympathy or Enthusiasm*.

11. Ibid., p. 87.

12. Ibid., pp. 93–94.

Bibliography

Bailey, Stephen K. "A Structured Interaction Pattern for Harpsichord and Kazoo," *Public Administration Review*, 14, no. 3 (1954), 202–205.

Baumgartner, John Stanley. *Project Management*. Homewood, Ill.: Irwin, 1963.

Bennis, Warren G. "The Coming Death of Bureaucracy." In David I. Clelland and William R. King, *Systems, Organizations, Analysis, Management*. New York: McGraw-Hill, 1969, pp. 12–18.

———. "Post-Bureaucratic Leadership," *Trans-Action* (July–August 1969), 44.

———, and Philip E. Slater. *The Temporary Society*. New York: Harper & Row, 1968.

Benson, Charles S., and Peter B. Lund. *Neighborhood Distribution of Local Public Services*. Berkeley, Calif.: Institute of Government Studies, University of California, Berkeley, 1969.

Biller, Robert J. "Converting Knowledge into Action: Toward a Postindustrial Society." In Jong S. Jun and William B. Storm, eds., *Tomorrow's Organizations: Challenges and Strategies*. Glenview, Ill.: Scott, Foresman, 1973.

Black, Henry Campbell. *Black's Law Dictionary*, 4th edition. St. Paul, Minn.: West, 1957.

Blau, Peter M. *Exchange and Power in Social Life*. New York: John Wiley & Sons, 1964.

———, and Charles H. Page. *Bureaucracy in Modern Society*. New York: Random House, 1956.

Brandl, John. "Public Service Education in the 1970s," School of Public Affairs, University of Minnesota, Mimeo, January 1976, pp. 1–14.

Buchanan, James W., and Gordon Tullock. *The Calculus of Consent*. Ann Arbor: University of Michigan Press, 1962.

Caldwell, Lynton K. "Thomas Jefferson and Public Administration." *Public Administration Review*, 3, no. 3 (1943). Reprinted in Claude E. Hawley and Ruth G. Weintraub, *Administration Questions and Political Answers*. New York: D. Van Nostrand Co., 1966, pp. 7–15.

Chapman, Richard, and Frederic N. Cleaveland. *Meeting the Needs of Tomorrow's Public Service: Guidelines for Professional Education in Public Administration*. Washington, D.C.: National Academy of Public Administration, 1973.

Charlesworth, James C., ed. *The Theory and Practice of Public Administration: Scope, Objectives, and Methods*. Philadelphia: The American Academy of Political and Social Science, October 1968.

Chitwood, Stephen R. "Social Equity and Social Service Productivity," *Public Administration Review*, 34 (January–February 1974), 29–35.

Clelland, David I., and William R. King. *Systems Analysis and Project Management*. New York: McGraw-Hill, 1968.

————. *Systems, Organizations, Analysis, Management: A Book of Readings*. New York: McGraw-Hill, 1969.

Cleveland, Harlan. *The Future Executive: A Guide for Tomorrow's Managers*. New York: Harper & Row, 1972.

Committee for Economic Development. *Reshaping Government in Metropolitan Areas*. New York: Committee for Economic Development, 1970.

Crain, G. Robert, Elihu Katz, and D. B. Rosenthal. *The Politics of Community Conflict*. Indianapolis: Bobbs-Merrill, 1969.

Crozier, Michel. *The Bureaucratic Phenomenon*. Chicago: The University of Chicago Press, 1964.

Cyert, Richard, and James March. *A Behavioral Theory of the Firm*. Englewood Cliffs, N.J.: Prentice-Hall, 1963.

Davis, James, and Kenneth Dolbeare. *Little Groups of Neighbors: The Selective Service System*. Chicago: Markham Press, 1968.

Downs, Anthony. *An Economic Theory of Democracy*. New York: Harper & Row, 1957.

————. *Inside Bureaucracy*. Boston: Little, Brown, 1967.

Drucker, Peter. *The Age of Discontinuity: Guidelines to a Changing Society*. New York: Harper & Row, 1969.

Etzioni, Amitai. *A Comparative Analysis of Complex Organizations*. New York: The Free Press, 1961.

————. "Mixed Scanning: A 'Third' Approach to Decision-Making." *Public Administration Review*, 27, no. 5 (December 1967), 386–387.

————. *Modern Organizations*. Englewood Cliffs, N. J.: Prentice-Hall, 1964.

Fesler, James. *Area and Administration*. University, Ala.: University of Alabama Press, 1949.

Frederickson, H. George. *Neighborhood Control in the 1970s*. New York: Chandler Publishing Co., 1973.

————, ed. "Curriculum Essays on Citizens, Politics and Administration in Urban Neighborhoods." *Public Administration Review*, Special Issue, 32 (November 1972).

Frederickson, H. George, and Linda Schluter O'Leary. *Power, Public Opinion, and Policy in a Metropolitan Community: A Case Study of Syracuse, New York*. New York: Praeger Publishers, 1973.

Frederickson, H. George, and Charles R. Wise, eds., *Public Administration and Public Policy*. Lexington, Mass.: Lexington Books, 1977.

Gawthrop, Louis C. *Administrative Politics and Social Change*. New York: St. Martin's Press, 1971.

Gore, William J. *Administrative Decision-Making: A Heuristic Model*. New York: John Wiley & Sons, 1964.

Griggs v. *Duke Power Co.*, 401 U.S., 424, 433 (March 7, 1971).

Hardin, Charles M. *Food and Fiber in American Politics*. Washington, D.C.: U.S. Government Printing Office, 1968.

Harris, T. George. "Organic Populism: A Conversation with Warren G. Bennis." *Psychology Today* (February 1970), 48.

Hart, David K. "Social Equity, Justice and the Equitable Administrator." *Public Administration Review*, 34 (January–February 1974), 6.

————, and William G. Scott. "The Moral Nature of Man in Organizations: A Comparative Analysis." *The Academy of Management Journal*, 14, no. 2 (June 1971), 241–255.

Hawkins v. *Town of Shaw*, 427 F.2d 1286 (5th Cir. 1971) aff'd 461 F.2d 1171 (1972) (en banc).

Honey, John C. "A Report: Higher Education for Public Service." *Public Administration Review*, 27 (November 1967), 294–321.

Ink, Dwight. "A Management Crisis for the New President: People Programs." *Public Administration Review*, 28, no. 6 (November–December 1968), 546–552.

Jencks, Christopher et al. *Inequality: A Reassessment of the Effect of Family and Schooling in America*. New York: Basic Books, 1972.

Jun, Jong S., and William B. Storm, eds. *Tomorrow's Organizations: Challenges and Strategies*. Glenview, Ill.: Scott, Foresman, 1973.

Katz, Daniel, and Robert Kahn. *The Social Psychology of Organizations*. New York: John Wiley & Sons, 1966.

Kaufman, Herbert. "Administrative Decentralization and Political Power." *Public Administration Review*, 29 (January–February 1969), 3–15.

———. *Are Government Organizations Immortal?* Washington, D.C.: The Brookings Institution, 1976.

Kirkhart, Larry. "Public Administration and Selected Developments in Social Science: Toward a Theory of Public Administration." In Frank Marini, ed., *Toward a New Public Administration: The Minnowbrook Perspective*. San Francisco: Chandler Publishing Co., 1971, pp. 127–163.

Kotler, Milton. *Neighborhood Government: The Local Foundations of Political Life*. Indianapolis and New York: Bobbs-Merrill, 1969.

Kuhn, Thomas. *The Structure of Scientific Revolutions*. Chicago: University of Chicago Press, 1970.

Leys, Wayne A. R. *Ethics For Policy Decisions*. Englewood Cliffs, N.J.: Prentice-Hall, 1952.

Likert, Rensis. *The Human Organization: Its Management and Value*. New York: McGraw-Hill, 1967.

———. *New Patterns of Management*. New York: McGraw-Hill, 1961.

Lindbloom, Charles. *The Intelligence of Democracy: Decision-Making through Mutual Adjustment*. New York: Free Press, 1965.

Lineberry, Robert L., and Edmund P. Fowler. "Reformism and Public Policies in American Cities." *American Political Science Review*, 67 (September 1967), 702.

Lowi, Theodore J. *The End of Liberalism*. New York: W. W. Norton & Co., 1969.

Maass, Arthur. *Muddy Waters*. Cambridge, Mass.: Harvard University Press, 1951.

McCurdy, Howard E. *Public Administration: A Bibliography*. Washington, D.C.: The College of Public Affairs, The American University, 1972.

McGregor, Eugene B. "Social Equity and the Public Service." *Public Administration Review*, 34 (January–February 1974), 23–24.

March, James, and Herbert Simon. *Organizations*. New York: John Wiley & Sons, 1958.

Marini, Frank, ed. *Toward a New Public Administration: The Minnowbrook Perspective*. San Francisco: Chandler Publishing Co., 1971.

Millett, John D. *Organization for the Public Service*. Princeton, N.J.: D. Van Nostrand Co., 1966.

Mosher, Frederick C. *Democracy and the Public Service*. New York: Oxford University Press, 1968.

———. *Governmental Reorganizations: Cases and Commentary*. Indianapolis: Bobbs-Merrill, 1967.

Ostrom, Vincent. *The Intellectual Crisis in American Public Administration*. University, Ala.: University of Alabama Press, 1973.

———, Charles Tiebout, and Robert Warren. "The Organization of Government in Metropolitan Areas: A Theoretical Inquiry," *American Political Science Review,* 61 (December 1961), 831–842.

Perrow, Charles. *Complex Organizations: A Critical Essay*. Glenview, Ill.: Scott, Foresman, 1972.

Perry, David. "The Suburb as a Model for Neighborhood Control." In George Frederickson, *Neighborhood Control in the 1970s*. New York: Chandler Publishing Co., 1973, pp. 85–100.

Pfiffner, John, and Frank Sherwood. *Administrative Organization*. Englewood Cliffs, N.J.: Prentice-Hall, 1960.

Porter, David O., and Teddy Wood Porter. "Social Equity and Fiscal Federalism." *Public Administration Review*, 34 (January–February 1974), 36–43.

Pressman, Jeffrey L., and Aaron Wildavsky. *Implementation*. Berkeley, Calif.: University of California Press, 1973.

Presthus, Robert. *The Organizational Society*. New York: Alfred A. Knopf, 1962.

Price, Don. "1984 and Beyond: Social Engineering or Political Values." In Frederick C. Mosher, ed., *American Public Administration: Past, Present, Future*. University, Ala.: University of Alabama Press, 1975, pp. 233–252.

"Public Service Education in the 1970s." School of Public Affairs, University of Minnesota, Mimeo. January 1976, p. 2.

Rawls, John. *A Theory of Justice*. Cambridge, Mass.: The Belknap Press of Harvard University Press, 1971.

Reed, William H. "The Decline of the Hierarchy in Industrial Organizations." In David I. Clelland and William R. King, *Systems, Organizations, Analysis, Management*. New York: McGraw-Hill, 1969, pp. 22–29.

Riker, William H. *Federalism: Origin, Operation, Significance*. Boston: Little, Brown, 1964.

Rodriguez v. *San Antonio*, U.S. Supreme Court, March 21, 1972.

Roethlisberger, F. J., and W. J. Dickson. *Management and the Worker*. Cambridge, Mass.: Harvard University Press, 1939.

Rourke, Frances E. *Bureaucracy, Politics and Public Policy*. 2d ed. Boston: Little, Brown, 1976.

Schott, Richard L. "Public Administration as a Profession: Problems and Prospects," *Public Administration Review* 36, no. 3 (May–June 1976), 253–259.

Schultze, Charles L. *The Politics and Economics of Public Spending*. Washington, D.C.: The Brookings Institution, 1969.

Scott, William G., and David K. Hart. *Organizational America*. Boston: Houghton Mifflin Co., 1979.

Serrano v. *Priest*, 487 P2d 1241 (1972).

Simon, Herbert. *Administrative Behavior*. New York: Macmillan Co., 1957.

———. *Models of Man*. New York: John Wiley & Sons, 1956.

Steiner, George A., and William G. Ryan. *Industrial Project Management*. New York: Macmillan Co., 1968.

Stone, Alice, and Donald Stone. "Appendix: Case Histories of Early Professional Education Programs." In Frederick C. Mosher, ed., *American Public Administration: Past, Present, Future*. University, Ala.: University of Alabama Press, 1975, pp. 268–290.

"Symposium on Productivity in Government." *Public Administration Review*, 32 (November–December 1972), pp. 739–851.

Thompson, James D. *Organizations in Action: The Social Science Bases of Administrative Theory*. New York: McGraw-Hill, 1967.

Thompson, Victor A. *Modern Organization*. New York: Alfred A. Knopf, 1961.

———. *Without Sympathy or Enthusiasm*. University, Ala.: University of Alabama Press, 1975.

Viteritti, Joseph P. *Bureaucracy and Social Justice*. Port Washington, N.Y.: Kennikat Press, 1979.

Waldo, Dwight. "Developments in Public Administration." *Annals of the American Academy of Political and Social Science,* 404 (November 1972), 217–245.

——. *Public Administration in a Time of Turbulence.* San Francisco: Chandler Publishing Co., 1971.

——. "Scope of the Theory of Public Administration." In James C. Charlesworth, ed., *Theory and Practice of Public Administration: Scope, Objectives and Methods.* Philadelphia: The American Academy of Political and Social Science, October 1968, pp. 1–26.

Weber, Max. *The Theory of Social and Economic Organization.* Translated by A. M. Henderson and Talcott Parsons. Fair Lawn, N.J.: Oxford University Press, 1947.

White, Leonard D. *Introduction to the Study of Public Administration.* New York: Macmillan Co., 1926.

Whyte, William H., Jr. *The Organization Man.* Garden City, N.Y.: Doubleday, 1956.

Wilcox, Herbert. "The Cultural Traits of Hierarchy in Middle Class Children." *Public Administration Review,* 29 (March–April 1968), 222–235.

Wildavsky, Aaron. *The Politics of the Budgetary Process.* Boston: Little, Brown, 1974.

Wilson, Woodrow. "The Study of Public Administration." *Political Science Quarterly,* 2, no. 1 (June 1887), as reprinted in 56 (December 1941), 493–507.

Woll, Peter. *Public Policy.* Cambridge, Mass.: Winthrop Publishers, 1974.

Index